# GEORGE RATCLIFFE

Among books by the same author:

*Cana Revisited – a personal pilgrimage* (1994)

*To Be a Christian* (1994)

*Ghost Stories of a Norfolk Parson* (1986)

# GEORGE RATCLIFFE WOODWARD

## 1848–1934

*Priest, Poet, and Musician*

by

JOHN E. BARNES

The Canterbury Press
Norwich

© The Theodore Trust 1996

First Published 1996 by The Canterbury Press Norwich
(a publishing imprint of Hymns Ancient & Modern Limited,
a registered charity)
St Mary's Works, St Mary's Plain,
Norwich, Norfolk, NR3 3BH

British Library Cataloguing in Publication Data

A catalogue record for this book is available
from the British Library

ISBN 1-85311-127-9

*Typeset by David Gregson Associates, Beccles, Suffolk
Printed and bound in Great Britain by
Antony Rowe Ltd, Chippenham, Wiltshire*

# CONTENTS

# SOURCES AND ACKNOWLEDGEMENTS

In the late nineteenth-thirties Athelstan Riley published a short appreciation of G. R. Woodward's life and work. It is very brief – a single folded sheet – undated, and it contains several minor inaccuracies. It may perhaps have been produced for circulation among members of one of the bodies with which Woodward was associated, such as the Plainsong and Mediaeval Music Society, and it also seems to have been inserted at the back of at least some of the subsequently-printed copies of *The Cowley Carol Book*, Woodward's best-known work. More recently, in 1985, Mervyn Horder published a fuller study in the *Bulletin of The Hymn Society*. This naturally pays particular attention to Woodward's achievements as a writer and translator of hymns and carols, and as the compiler of a hymnal and of various carol collections.

Useful material is to be found in Dom Anselm Hughes' *Septuagesima, Reminiscences of the Plainsong & Mediaeval Music Society*, published in 1959, and in the book *The Music of Charles Wood – A Critical Study* which Ian Copley published in 1978. There is also a paragraph about Woodward in Colin Stephenson's *Walsingham Way*, 1970, although this unfortunately contains several inaccuracies and makes some rather dubious assumptions.

Towards the end of his life, Woodward himself wrote some brief autobiographical notes, which provide a certain amount of information about his family and schooling, but unfortunately the notes do not extend beyond his years at Harrow. I was allowed to transcribe them, together with two letters written to Woodward by his father, when they were in the possession of his late great-step-nephew, James Horsfall, who died in 1988. Mr Horsfall allowed me to visit Woodward's former home in Highgate, and gave me reminiscences of his visits there as a boy. He also allowed me to make copies of some of the very few photographs of Woodward which exist. I am most grateful to him, as I am to his niece Mrs Ann Duff, who allowed me to see the three manuscript sermons and one speech which are now in her possession, together with further letters to Woodward from his father and a number of letters from his half-sister, besides certain other letters and papers.

There are a number of other people who have given me help and encouragement, and to whom I am very grateful. In particular I must mention Mr John Creasey, Librarian of Dr Williams' Library, London, who has provided me with a great deal of information in the course of several years. Others include The Revd Timothy Bugby, Vicar of St Augustine's, Highgate; Miss Catherine Gurney, a great-grandaughter of Canon Henry James Lee Warner, who provided me with information concerning the Lee Warner family; The Lord Horder; Fr Graham Leonard, formerly Bishop of London; Miss Margaret Lowen; Dr Roy Massey; The Revd David Newton, Rector of Chelmondiston; Mr Cameron Pyke; Dr Watkins Shaw; Mr Howard Thomas; Mr Roy Tricker; Mr John Wilson; Sir David Willcocks; Mr Derek Williams; and the late Mr Edward Wood and the late Miss J. K. S. Wood, the son and daughter of the composer Charles Wood.

I am also grateful to members of staff at The British Library, The College of Arms, Gonville and Caius College Library, Cambridge, King's Lynn Public Library, Lambeth Palace Library, The Liverpool Record Office, The National Gallery, London, The Norwich Diocesan Registry, and The Suffolk Record Office.

J.E.B.

# INTRODUCTION

' ... we shall be as though we had never been ... our
names will be forgotten with the passing of time, and no
one will remember anything we did.'
*Wisdom of Soloman 2.2,4*

The name of G. R. Woodward is unlikely to be forgotten,
because most probably it will continue to appear in the standard hymn and carol books beneath such popular items as
'DING DONG! MERRILY ON HIGH' and 'THIS JOYFUL EASTERTIDE'.
And of course it will continue to be possible for students to
discover the dates of his birth and death, the names of the
places where he lived and worked, and the titles and contents
of his publications. But it could easily happen that little more
than these somewhat bare bones will survive. George
Ratcliffe Woodward died in 1934, and even sixty years after
a death more personal information about an individual has
begun to vanish. Papers have become lost or destroyed,
books and other possessions have been dispersed, friends and
contemporaries have died, and those who retain any first-
hand recollection of a person are few and perhaps difficult to
discover. And all this is more especially the case if the individual in question has lived to a fairly advanced age, has led
a quiet and secluded life away from public office and events,
and has furthermore been survived by no close relatives.

Such was the case with G. R. Woodward, the subject of
this study, and the writer believes that unless an account of
his life is written now, before further information is lost, then
any future account may consist of little more than a list of
the more obvious names and dates – the depiction of a
skeleton rather than of a person. Already there are many
questions which cannot be answered, and for certain periods
in Woodward's life the information which remains is very
limited indeed.

Of course there are many writers of popular hymns and
carols about whom we know little, and the mere fact that a
handful out of the considerable number of hymns and carols

1

which Woodward composed or translated have become well-known is not in itself a sufficient reason for his life and work to be recorded. Whenever a study such as this is proposed, the would-be writer must ask at the outset whether the life and work of the subject is genuinely significant and interesting, and whether it continues to have the ability to illuminate, edify, and entertain. But whilst it is proper to ask these questions, the answers to them will always to some extent be subjective. In the present case, some, like myself, will find Woodward an intriguing and appealing figure, well worthy of recording, and this not least as a vignette from a literary and religious world which is infinitely more remote than the sixty years since his death would suggest. To us, the part which he played in the revival of Plainchant, in the popularisation of carols, in the preservation and presentation of ancient tunes, in the enrichment of hymnody, – these things will seem significant. Likewise the places with which he was especially associated, Cambridge, Pimlico, Walsingham, Highgate, may add particular interest, whilst his dry humour may appeal and his involvement in things as diverse as bee-keeping and printing may excite curiosity. But to others, I readily accept, he will emerge as a person whose interests, outlook, and sympathies were unacceptably narrow, and whose limitations of mind and heart were all too apparent. His long life was lived out in a fairly small world, and this largely of his own choosing. To some of the relatively few people who knew him he must have seemed eccentric and out of place in the world of the twentieth century. And so it must remain for the reader to decide whether or not a study such as this is justified and desirable. He or she may judge that the survival of just a handful of well-known hymns and carols such as those mentioned above is sufficient memorial. Or, on the other hand, that their author too – the priest, poet, and musician – deserves to be remembered.

CHAPTER ONE

# THE EARLY YEARS 1848–1869

Those who know of George Ratcliffe Woodward through his
carols, and are familiar with such lines as:

> Blest withouten match
> O Bethlehem, is the gable
> O'er that lowly cratch:-
> The crib within thy stable.[1]

and

> E'en so here below below,
> Let steeple-bells be swungen:
> And i-o, i-o, i-o,
> By priest and people sungen:[2]

may suspect that their writer felt an affinity with the past,
and had a somewhat romantic approach towards it. This is
suggested by his inclination to use the archaic word or
phrase, and by the pseudo-Mediaeval form and feeling which
he gives to many of his carols. Such a perception of
Woodward's character is reinforced by the opening of the
autobiographical notes which he wrote down in old age, and
which provide almost the only first-hand information now
available concerning his early years.[3] He begins these notes
by saying:

> The WOODWARDS are said to be found in the neighbour-
> hood of all the Royal Forests of England, e.g. The Forest of
> Deane. Our ancestors are said to come from Worcestershire,
> or according to one of my relations, from Warwickshire.
> Woodwards were settled in Worcestershire at Ripple,
> Hardwick, Besford Court, Birlingham, Bricklehampton, and
> later at Arley on Severn.[4] On the Bayeux Tapestry, one of
> Duke William's knights is displayed HIC EST WOODWARD ... On
> our grandmother Woodward's side, we are descended from
> Moll Davies, King Charles II's favourite, or rather one of
> them. She became by him the mother of Mary Tudor, who
> married the first Lord Derwenter. I believe that we are in
> direct line from Francis Radcliffe, brother of the noble
> James Ratcliffe, who was attained and beheaded after the
> 1715 turnout.

A norman knight, royal foresters, Worcestershire land-owners, a king's favourite, and the supremely romantic figure of James, Earl of Derwentwater. But all of this is some-what hazy – 'I believe ...', '... are said to'. And also some-what removed from the reality – albeit the prosperous reality – of nineteenth-century Liverpool. It seems that Woodward's grandfather, Thomas Woodward, came from Worcestershire to Liverpool – 'migrated', as Woodward says – in the early years of the century. He presumably came to seek his fortune in the rapidly expanding port, where he founded the firm of Robert and Thomas Woodward and Co., Cornmerchants. Who Robert was is not clear; perhaps he was a brother who followed Thomas to Liverpool and was taken into partner-ship. By the middle of the century, if not earlier, the firm was trading from 16 James Street, a site which, as Woodward remarks in his notes with characteristic humour, 'has been transformed into the mouth-piece, or bolt-hole, of the Mersey Tunnel'.

It would seem that the business establishment by Thomas Ratcliffe flourished, because when the first of the twelve children born to him and his wife Sarah Ratcliffe arrived on June 4th 1811, they were living in a fashionable part of the city, in a street adjoining Rodney Street, where W. E. Gladstone had been born two years previously. This eldest son was named George because he had been born on George III's birthday, and Ratcliffe after his mother's family. The Ratcliffes would appear to have been well established in the city, since Woodward remarks, again rather vaguely, that 'The Ratcliffes seem to have held office as Churchwardens etc. in Liverpool', giving the impression that his grandfather Thomas had perhaps married into an old-established merchant family. Apart from their claim to descend from the Derwentwater family, he relates no more about the Ratcliffes other than the facts that his grandmother was one of several sisters, the daughters of Thomas and Mary Ratcliffe, and that she had been brought up by her great-uncle, one Jonathan Ratcliffe.[5]

The elder George Ratcliffe Woodward entered his father's business 'against', his son wrote tersely, 'his inclinations', from which it appears that the corn trade held little interest

for him. Perhaps it would be revealing to know where his
true interests did lie, and whether they included religion,
music, poetry, the classics – the things which would be so
important to his son. To know this might be to discover a
possible influence on the young Woodward; as it is, there is
very little evidence as to how he acquired his life-long preoccupations. The father was to marry three times, George the
younger being the eldest son of the second marriage. His first
wife, Anne Jane Tyrer, was the only daughter of a Liverpool
shipowner named William Tyrer. We are told that they had
'several children', including a boy named William Ratcliffe
who died as a child in about 1855, and a daughter called
Annie who later married Capt. Hopton Scott Stewart and
was the mother of Violet Horsfall, Woodward's step-niece,
godchild, and heir. The fact that Woodward is so unspecific
about even the number of his half-brothers and sisters
suggests that he may have seen little of them, with the exception that is of Annie, who was brought up by James Tyrer,
presumably a brother of the first Mrs Woodward. In the
notes, he refers to 'Mr James Tyrer (whose memory I treasure
with gratitude and affectionate regard)', and in an undated
letter to Violet Horsfall, seemingly written towards the end
of his life, he refers to 'dear old Mr Tyrer, whose memory is
most dear to me', and adds that James Tyrer had been his
godfather.

The date of Anne Tyrer's death is not recorded in Woodward's notes, but this had occurred before March 1848 when
George Ratcliffe Woodward senior, then aged thirty-eight,
married his second wife, Anne Deville Owen, daughter of
John and Sarah Owen of Field House, Marchington, Staffordshire. The marriage took place in that county, but at Tixall,
the home of James Tyrer, rather than at Marchington. This
suggests that a close bond existed between the two brothers-
in-law, as does the fact that Tyrer, who was unmarried, both
brought up Annie and became Woodward's godfather. Many
years later Woodward appears to have still retained a particular affection for Staffordshire, the county which he must
have specially associated both with his mother and with his
godfather, and in a sermon which seems to date from the late
nineteen-twenties, he spoke of 'the banks of that ancient

river, the silver Trent, near Cannock Chase at the foot of the hill country of that beloved old county of Staffordshire'. Both Cannock Chase and the Trent lie close to Tixall.

The second marriage of George Ratcliffe Woodward senior took place in early March 1848, and on Wednesday December 27th of that year a first child was born and was named after his father. George and Anne Woodward were then living across the Mersey in Birkenhead, at 26 Hamilton Square. This square, which in the middle of the last century offered the best address in Birkenhead, is wide and spacious, and surrounded by large early nineteenth-century terraced houses. It was here that the birth took place, and a month later, on January 25th 1849, the child was taken across the water to Liverpool for baptism in the parish church, where the rite was performed by one of the assistant curates, the Revd J. B. Phillips.[6] A second son, Basil Hall, followed in March 1850, and in December 1851 Anne's last child, Sarah Helen Deville (known subsequently as Helen or Nellie) was born. The birth took place at Tixall – again suggesting a strong bond between the Woodwards and James Tyrer – and nine days later Anne died. Her body was buried in the churchyard at Tixall.

The younger George was just three years old at the time of his mother's death. He wrote in his autobiographical notes that his 'dear mother ... was deservedly loved & revered by all who ever saw her, and was truly said to be the model of all that is lovely and of good report'. For the next five years or so it seems that he and his brother and sister, 'we three orphans' as he calls them, were cared for by their two grand-mothers, both of whom were then living near Birkenhead. The Owens had apparently moved from Marchington to Claughton, and the Thomas Woodwards had left Liverpool for Rock Ferry. During the latter part of this period Woodward attended his first school, Miss Pennington's Day School at Rock Ferry. In about 1856, however, when he would have been eight, his father married for the third time. His bride was a Miss Eliza Sophia Bland, whose father Woodward describes as 'The Revd Robert Bland, a great scholar, & poet, tutor to Lord Byron, being one of the Masters at Harrow (The Grove was his house), and afterwards Rector of Kenilworth'. It is interesting that in these brief notes Woodward wishes to record – apparently thinking it significant – that his step-grandfather was 'a great scholar and poet', and one can only speculate as to whether the older man and his work had any appreciable influence upon the form which his own scholarship and poetry would take.

It appears that Woodward's father and step-mother now moved back into Lancashire to live at Advie House, Rainhill, then a rural area between Liverpool and St Helen's (they would later move again, to the Elms, Litherland), and that the children then left their grandparents to live with them. Leaving the school at Rock Ferry, Woodward records that he was next 'taught by a Miss Musgrove, who kept a boy's and girl's private school, hard by. This good lady knew little or no Latin at all. With the best intentions, she failed to teach me adequately: and I was never properly grounded. Also she gave me a distaste for books, by plunging me too early into difficult passages of Shakespeare. So much valuable time was lost in my early training.' These reflections on his education between the ages of eight and eleven are interesting, and seem to suggest some kind of lingering regret. Did the inadequate grounding in Latin and the 'distaste' for books perhaps make his time at his preparatory school memorably difficult? Or was there possibly a continuing hurt over the fact that he later failed to take a good degree at Cambridge, with an imagined need to somehow justify this?

At the ages of eleven and nine respectively, Woodward and his brother Basil were sent way to a preparatory school in Hertfordshire, at Elstree, run by the Revd L. J. Berneys. Again he was not uncritical of the establishment, remarking that 'on looking back I must unwillingly confess that some of the under-masters were hardly up to the mark: also we were kept on rather short commons, & had not even enough water to drink'. This last assertion sounds surprising, but Athelstan Riley, who used the autobiographical notes when compiling his brief appreciation of Woodward's life and work in the late nineteen-thirties, comments that 'it is a fact that at this period drinking was looked upon as bad for boys, and was severely curtailed'.[7] But despite the inadequacies of

the under-masters and of the food and drink, he records that
the Revd Thompson Podmore, who took over the school
when Berneys became Rector of Great Stanmore, and who
Riley calls 'a schoolmaster of some celebrity' took 'much
pains over my Latin and Greek', and probably thereby laid
the foundations for both his later successes in the Classics at
public school, and his lifelong interest in classical literature.
He also notes that he 'rose to be head of the school', which
would seem to testify both to his character and personality at
that time, and he observed that 'The Elstree boys, on the
whole, were very good fellows, gentle men, and with some of
them I have kept up to the present date, but many have fallen
asleep', this long association with his former companions
seeming to suggest his sociability.

Of his public school, Harrow, Woodward had no criticism
(other than of one particular master); his five years there
from 1863 onwards seem to have been a particularly happy
time – 'I received nothing but kindness from my masters
there. Nor can I ever repay the debt that I owe to my tutors
there, from the first to last' – and he maintained an intense
loyalty to the school for the rest of his life. It was almost
inevitable that Harrow should have been chosen for him: his
stepmother's father had been a house master there and the
Revd 'Ben' Drury, whose house he entered, was her cousin;
in addition, one of the assistant masters, G. F. Harris, was a
relative of his father. The school would also have
commended itself however by its own qualities; Canon G. L.
Prestige has written of Harrow enjoying at this time 'a period
of exceptional prosperity under Dr Butler'.[8] The one master
he disliked (although disliked is perhaps too strong a term –
Woodward himself says 'the one I cared for least') was the
Revd B. F. Westcott (1825–1901), later well-known as a
considerable biblical scholar and distinguished Bishop of
Durham. He recalled that Westcott, who had examined him
and placed him when he entered the school, 'would not
have House-singing, absented himself from Lord's Cricket
Ground on the Eton & Harrow, and corrected my exercises
rather sneeringly, & not like the other masters'. The notes
do not mention Westcott's subsequent fame, and it is
tempting to see Woodward's view of him as being coloured

by a later distaste for Westcott's somewhat liberal views. However Professor V. H. Stanton has written of him that 'for the work of an ordinary form-master he was not well fitted. He did not understand the ordinary boy and he had difficulty in maintaining discipline'.[9] Cricket, in which Westcott apparently showed little interest, was to be a continuing enthusiasm in the case of Woodward, and in years to come he was rarely absent from the Eton and Harrow match.[10] Whilst a pupil he played in his house cricket eleven as well as in the football eleven, and nearly seventy years later he still remembered with disappointment, and with typical humility, that when one Fred Ponsonby had wanted to get him into the school eleven in 1868, on the strength of his bowling, he had failed because 'there were better bats, fielders, and bowlers'.

One surprising feature of Woodward's albeit brief account of his time at Harrow is the omission of any mention of the music master, John Farmer, who appears to have had a profound and lasting influence upon him. John Farmer (1836–1901), who was born at Nottingham and who had studied at Leipzig and taught at Zurich before joining the staff at Harrow in 1862, was a charismatic figure, extremely popular with his pupils, and an early figure in the revival of interest in the music of J. S. Bach. Bernaar Rainbow has written of him as a master at Harrow that 'resisting an academic approach, he showed the boys that massed singing was enjoyable, writing many songs for them that celebrated events in school life, introducing lighthearted songs, glees, and partsongs, and instituting house singing'.[11] In 1924 Woodward wrote to Archbishop Randall Davidson (1848–1930), who had been his contemporary at Harrow, 'It was John Farmer (whom our beloved and revered Dr Butler brought to Harrow) who first taught me to admire Palestrina & Bach & to study & love good Church music'.[12] It would seem that Woodward shared in the general liking of Farmer, and so disapproved of Westcott for opposing the house singing which Farmer had introduced, besides gaining from him the general interest in church music and the particular interest in J. S. Bach and in choral singing which would remain with him for the rest of his life.

Randall Davidson was not the only Harrovian of Woodward's day who would achieve distinction in the established Church, for another near-contemporary was Charles Gore (1853–1932) who became successively Bishop of Worcester, Birmingham, and Oxford, and was founder of The Community of the Resurrection. He joined the school in 1866, three years after Woodward, and like him came to venerate the distinguished headmaster of the day, Dr Henry Montagu Butler (1833–1918), of whom he wrote after Butler's death 'the memory of him is pure, gracious, and beautiful, without any flaw or counteracting bitterness'.[13] But whilst Gore was already a high churchman when he entered Harrow, and gathered around him there a high church 'set' which included G. W. E. Russell and others, it is unlikely that Woodward derived his Anglo-catholicism from this particular source. Quite apart from the fact that Woodward was five years his senior in age, Gore and his friends were attracted to liberal ideas and were admirers of Gladstone – things which were always anathema to Woodward – besides which Gore, unlike Woodward, was a great admirer of B. F. Westcott. As indeed was Davidson, who recalled that he had found Westcott's teaching 'a constant source of interest and gain'.[14] It is significant that Gore, although a prominent Anglo-catholic, is not mentioned in Woodward's autobiographical notes, nor indeed anywhere else in his writings. Woodward may, however, have made friends at Harrow with Walter Leaf (1852–1927), who was to become a distinguished classical scholar and banker, and who, like Gore, entered the school in 1866. Both men shared an interest in music, and in later years made translations from the *Greek Anthology*.[15] A book of Leaf's Greek translations inscribed 'G. R. Woodward, from Walter Leaf' which came to light some years ago in a second-hand bookshop in London certainly indicates that they were friends in later years, and their friendship may well have dated back to their time at Harrow and at Cambridge, where they again overlapped.

Academically, Mr. Podmore's 'much pains' over his Latin and Greek at Elstree seem to have borne fruit, because at Harrow Woodward won the Latin Alcaic Prize in 1867, in what he describes as 'a poor exercise', and in the following year the Greek Iambic Prize, besides being runner-up for four other prizes. His academic proficiency was sufficient for Dr Butler to secure for him one of the Sayer Scholarships to Cambridge. These two scholarships, worth fifty guineas a year for four years, had been founded by John Sayer in 1829 'for the promotion of classical learning and taste', and were open to boys from Harrow provided that they entered and resided at Gonville and Caius College. And so when he left school in 1869 Woodward had behind him a creditable, even if not brilliant, record both in the classroom and on the games field. So much we can deduce from the information which he provides in his notes. But nothing is revealed there as regards his thinking, ambitions, hopes, and feelings during the early years of his life. Sensitivity is certainly suggested by his long-remembered resentment of B. F. Westcott's manner when correcting his exercises. But there is a reticence about revealing the workings of his mind, soul, and heart. These remained – and would largely continue to remain – hidden.

CHAPTER TWO

# CAMBRIDGE AND PIMLICO
# 1869–1882

Woodward's autobiographical notes discontinue at the point
when he left Harrow, and although they did not record a
great deal more than the principal names, dates, and events
of his early years, they certainly provided rather more information than is available for the years which followed. As
regards Cambridge, no more survives than a handful of very
bare facts. According to Venn's *Biographical History of
Gonville and Caius College*, he was admitted a pensioner, as
a Sayer Scholar, on November 1st 1867, his scholarship
running from Lady Day 1869 to Lady Day 1872. He gradu-
ated in the latter year, with a third class in the Classical
Tripos.[1] And that is all. The silence, however, is almost
absolute as regards the two years between his leaving
Cambridge in 1872 and his ordination to the diaconate in
1874. His great-step-nephew, James Horsfall, remembered
that when he was a boy Woodward had given him a bicycle
on which he, Woodward, had cycled to Rome as a young
man. It is possible that this expedition took place during
those two unrecorded years. Certainly, and perhaps surprisingly for a high churchman, there seems to be no suggestion
that he attended a theological college prior to ordination,
despite the fact that a number of such institutions were in
existence by the 1870s; Chichester Theological College, for
example, having been founded as early as 1839.

That there is so little information about the five years
between his leaving Harrow in 1869 and his being ordained
in 1874 is particularly regrettable because it was most probably during this period that one of his principal and lifelong
preoccupations was formed, and it would be interesting to
know what particular influences were shaping his thinking.
When he went up to Cambridge his interest in the classical
languages and in church music were already in the process of
formation. The first had been awakened by the able and
enthusiastic teaching which he had received at his prepara-

tory and public schools, and, having pursued this interest further at university, it would remain with him for the future, and indeed have a particular manifestation in the small booklets of translations from the Greek classics which he produced in the last few years of his life. Similarly his interest in church music had been aroused during his school-days, most especially through the influence of John Farmer at Harrow. The seed of his interest in the translation and composition of verse, and most particularly of verse to be sung as hymns and carols may possibly have been sown by the school songs which Farmer composed, but this interest would not become manifest until some years later. However the preoccupation which must have been formed during this period – interest is hardly the right word – was religion, and religion in the form of Anglo-catholicism.

That he had become a committed Anglo-catholic during the five years between school and ordination is made plain by the fact than when he came to be made deacon in 1874, it was to serve as Assistant Curate at a London church which was renowned, even notorious, for its 'extreme' teaching and ritual. It is surprising that in the autobiographical notes, which Woodward wrote as an elderly and devout priest, there is no mention at all of religion. He does not record his baptism, and more surprisingly still he makes no mention of his confirmation, which presumably took place whilst he was a pupil at Harrow. Surely, one might think, his confirmation seemed more significant, if only in retrospect, than his playing in the house elevens? Perhaps this omission can be accounted for by the principle of 'reserve' in speaking about religious matters: a reserve which was not only in accord with the English character but which was also advocated as a matter of principle by the thinkers of the nineteenth-century Catholic revival within the Church of England. None the less, it may be that the absence of any reference to religion in the notes indicates that when he came up to Cambridge it was with that somewhat formal and conventional religion which was common to so many in the age and social class to which he belonged, despite Canon Prestige's assertion that the religious tradition of Harrow during his time there was 'definitely evangelical'.[2]

Perhaps it was at Cambridge that he first encountered Anglo-catholicism, and espoused the religious principles and convictions to which he adhered so faithfully and tenaciously for the rest of his life. But precisely where or from whom he imbibed those principles which would lead him to a curacy in the extreme and controversial parish of St Barnabas Pimlico, is not clear. In the 1870s there was no church in Cambridge which offered quite the 'advanced' form of Anglican teaching and worship with which he would become familiar in London. The one which came nearest to it was probably St Clement's, and it is possible that Woodward may have come under the influence of one of the curates there, the Revd E. G. Wood, who was Assistant Curate of St Clement's 1865–1885 and Vicar 1885–1930, and who in 1885 published a book entitled *Altar Lights and Eucharistic Vestments*, explaining their significance and advocating their use. Again it is possible that Woodward may have come into contact with the Cambridgeshire branch of the English Church Union, which had been founded in 1862 and was an Anglo-catholic society which he certainly supported later in life. It is also possible that he belonged to the Confraternity of the Most Holy Trinity (S.T.C.), which existed at this time as an Anglo-catholic devotional society for undergraduates and sympathetic dons.[3] Certainly Cambridge had not been immune to the effects of the Anglo-catholic revival which had been initiated in Oxford in the 1830s, and there were obviously individuals in Cambridge who had been deeply influenced by the teachings of the ninety *Tracts for the Times* which had been issued between 1833 and 1841, and which provided the movement with one of its names. Indeed Cambridge had made its own distinctive and significant contribution to the revival as a whole by means of the Cambridge Camden Society which was founded in 1839 to promote the study of ancient ecclesiastical buildings, and which before long came to lay down strict rules not only about what 'correctly' restored and newly built churches should look like, but also about how they should be furnished and what kind of services should take place within them.[4] It might be said in broad terms that the Oxford Movement and the Cambridge Camden Society complemented each other, the one being concerned with doctrine and spirituality and the other with the architectural and liturgical expression of those things. When Woodward came to Cambridge in 1869 it was thirty years since the foundation of the Society, and to a large extent it had run its course by then. Such activities of the Society as continued had gravitated to London, and its once highly influential journal *The Ecclesiologist* had ceased publication in the previous year. One of the co-founders of the Society had been the Revd Dr John Mason Neale (1818–1866), a renowned scholar and one of the most liturgically 'advanced' of the earlier Anglo-catholics. In time he was to have a profound influence on Woodward, who, it seems, came to see him as a kind of 'role-model'. However Neale cannot have had any direct influence upon Woodward during his years as an undergraduate since he had left Cambridge in 1842, and had died three years before Woodward entered the University. Nevertheless Woodward wrote in 1919 that 'for more than half a century I have been an enthusiastic lover and admirer of John Mason Neale's hymns of the Eastern Church',[5] which certainly suggests that his acquaintance with Neale's work began during this early period. But whether this acquaintance played an particular part in his coming to embrace Anglo-catholicism is unknown

If Woodward's distinctive religious views were first formed during the years between Harrow and his ordination, it would seem that this was also the time when his incipient interest in church music underwent an important development. In the letter to Archbishop Davidson which has already been quoted, he said that he owed his appreciation of Palestrina and J. S. Bach to his music master at Harrow; in another letter, written to his friend the composer Charles Wood (1866–1926) in the previous year, 1923, he had said, 'I am very glad you are harmonising some of the ordinary of the Mass; I am sure you know how to phrase it perfectly well. The Sanctus you have chosen is a great favourite of mine, now for exactly fifty years since I first heard it'.[6] Here, in claiming to have known a particular plainsong Sanctus for 'exactly' fifty years, Woodward is implying that he had become acquainted with plainsong by the year 1873, which was the year following his going down from Cambridge. It would be of interest to know where and when that acquaintance was made. Possibly it was at Cambridge during his time as an undergraduate: St Giles' Church had a strong musical tradition, and its moderately ritualistic worship may well have included the use of plainsong. Alternatively, it is possible that he may have encountered it on the continent during the two years which preceded his ordination and in which his movements are unknown. Again, he may have discovered plainsong at St Margaret's Church in his native Liverpool, where, from 1869 a person who would become both an authority on plainsong and a lifelong friend, was Assistant Curate. Whichever, it would remain a particular interest.

With his special interests within the fields of religion and music already established, Woodward was ordained deacon by the Bishop of London in December 1874. The following day, December 22nd, he received a letter from The Revd Charles Parnell, first Vicar of St Margaret's, Princes Road, Liverpool, which he kept, and which was still in his possession at the time of his death sixty years later. Parnell wrote:

> Dear Mr. Woodward,
>     We asked the prayers of the Church for you yesterday. We were all very glad to hear you had passed the Bishop's examination. You have chosen a very arduous path in life especially in these dark days but God will reward you for your generosity by supporting you with His grace.
>
>     May He enable you to gather a large harvest of souls into His garner. God bless you.
>
> Yrs. very faithfully,
>
> Charles Parnell[7]

This letter is interesting insofar as it establishes that Woodward had a link with what had become the leading Anglo-catholic church in Liverpool following its consecration five years earlier, and one which would shortly become well-known due to the prosecution of Parnell's successor, Fr Bell Cox, for committing ritualistic 'offences' under the Public Worship Regulation Act of 1874. St Margaret's, which was designed by G. E. Street – an architect whose work

Woodward would encounter again at Walsingham – had been founded by Robert Horsfall, a member of a family which was prominent in nineteeth-century Liverpool, producing both Lord Mayors and Members of Parliament for the city. The Horsfalls, like the Tyrers, were ship-owners, and were certainly known to the Woodwards, since in an undated letter to his step-niece Violet (who had herself married into the Horsfall family), Woodward mentioned that he shared a birthday with Jessie Horsfall, and had eaten a birthday lunch with her in 1858, when he was ten and she was five. It is possible, of course, that Robert Horsfall may have played a part in Woodward's 'discovery' of Anglo-catholicism, or that he may at least have encouraged it.

Churches such as St Margaret's, Liverpool, were in a sense successors to the London church which Woodward was ordained to serve at as Assistant Curate, St Barnabas', Pimlico. For St Barnabas', consecrated nearly twenty years earlier in 1850, claims to be the first church to be built and furnished specifically for the type of worship which expressed the teaching and aspirations of Anglo-catholicism. It had been founded (and largely paid for) by the Revd William James Earley Bennett, Vicar of St Paul's Knightsbridge, to serve that particularly poor and populous area on the edge of his parish which adjoined Belgravia, an area which one contemporary dubbed 'a deplorable slum' and a haunt 'of sin and brutal degradation'.[8] A College to provide accommodation for priests and others – the first Clergy House in the Church of England – was built in 1846, and in the following year Dr E. B. Pusey (1800–1882), a leader and in certain respects the backbone of the Oxford Movement, laid the foundation stone of the church, which was consecrated three years later. In the Octave of the Consecration sermons were preached by such key figures in the Anglo-catholic revival as Keble, Pusey, Neale, and Manning, and so the tradition in which the church was to stand was made perfectly clear from the beginning. From the outset the offices of Morning and Evening Prayer, together with the Holy Communion, were celebrated each day and St Barnabas' became the first church in which these services were sung daily. It is also claimed that this was the first

Anglican church in which the traditional liturgical colours
were used, the sign of the Cross made, and the traditional
eastward position adopted by the celebrant of the Holy
Communion service. It was, as one writer has called it, 'a
living embodiment of the ideals of the Oxford Movement'.[9]

But if St Barnabas' was a pioneer in the presentation of
Anglo-catholic worship, it was no less a pioneer in experi-
encing the opposition and persecution which such worship
often encountered in the second half of the nineteenth-
century. Riots began on November 10th in the year of the
church's consecration, and these were to continue until 1857.
*The Times* launched a campaign against the church, and it
was ridiculed in *Punch*. The Prime Minister, Lord John
Russell, spoke against it at a Lord Mayor's banquet, saying
that he would 'rather worship in the temple of Diana than in
the "painted Tabernacle" on the banks of the Thames'. At
the request of the Bishop of London, Bennett resigned in
March 1851, and was succeeded by the Revd James Skinner;
he was assisted by the Revd Charles Lowder, who, like
Bennett, was long remembered for both his work amongst
the poor and for his endurance of persecution. In 1866
Skinner was followed by the Revd George Cosby White, who
came to Pimlico from the incumbency of Wantage, and it was
he who offered Woodward a curacy at St Barnabas' in 1874,
two years before he left to become Vicar of Malvern Link in
Worcestershire.

St Barnabas' Pimlico was famed for its Anglo-catholic
teaching and worship and for the opposition which these
provoked, and it was to become no less famed for its music,
Lord Halifax writing in the course of time of 'the unsur-
passed and unsurpassable beauty of the music at St
Barnabas'. Bennett had a particular love of music, and a
choir school had formed part of his original foundation of St
Barnabas. Its boys were drawn largely from the sons of
country clergy, and the first Priest-Precentor was the distinguished nineteenth-century musician the Revd Sir Frederick
Gore Ouseley (1825–1889), who eventually took the choir
boys from Pimlico to his own new foundation at Tenbury
Wells, whereafter the St Barnabas' choir was made up of
local boys. Bennett had a great liking for plainsong, and

whilst this featured in the choral repertoire from the first, it came to hold a special place after the appointment of Thomas Helmore (1811–1890) as Honorary Precentor. Helmore, who had been Master of the Choristers at the Chapel Royal since 1846, has been described as a 'veteran champion of plainsong'. He edited various manuals of plainsong, and according to the Revd Francis Lloyd Bagshawe, who succeeded White as Vicar in 1876, 'it was at St Barnabas' that after a long silence of three centuries the ancient ecclesiastic music of the Church was restored to its proper place in our services'.[10] Many years later the writer of Woodward's obituary in the *Church Times* would speak of St Barnabas' as having been the place 'where the purest Plainsong could be heard'.

Besides having a special place in the history of the revival of plainsong, St Barnabas also has a particular place in the revival of hymnody. According to the anonymous writer of *The History of St Barnabas' Pimlico* published in 1933, 'Mr Bennett would not allow any of the existing hymn books in the church, on the grounds that they were all Protestant in tone',[11] and this led Helmore, in association with John Mason Neale, to produce the *Hymnal Noted* which appeared in two parts, in 1851 and 1854, and was made up of translations of the ancient office hymns. Later the compilation of *Hymns Ancient and Modern* was likewise associated with the church. White, the Vicar, was a member of the committee formed to bring it into being, as was Helmore, and the first meeting was held at St Barnabas' in January 1859.[12] Gore Ouseley and J. M. Neale gave the project their blessing, and when it was completed in 1861 it immediately came into use at St Barnabas', to be supplemented in Woodward's time by G. H. Palmer's *Hymner*. Later *The English Hymnal* would likewise be connected with the church through The Revd The Hon A. F. A. Hanbury Tracy, Vicar of St Barnabas' 1898–1927, being a member of the committee which compiled it – as was Woodward for a short time – and through Ralph Vaughan Williams, its musical editor, having briefly been organist at the church.

Woodward's enthusiasm for plainsong and for hymnody must undoubtedly have been stimulated by the tradition

which he found at St Barnabas', and in particular through
the influence of two people who would continue to play an
important part in his life. The one was The Revd George
Herbert Palmer (1846–1926). According to The History of
St Barnabas, it was Woodward who 'by his influence'
persuaded Palmer to come to the church as Priest-Organist in
1876, and this tends to confirm that Woodward had indeed
come to know Palmer during the years when the latter was
Assistant Curate at St Margaret's, Liverpool, a post which he
occupied from 1869 until 1876. They had not been contemporaries at Cambridge, Palmer having been an undergraduate at Trinity College from 1865 until 1869, the year in
which he went down and was ordained and Woodward came
up from Harrow. They may possibly have met in Cambridge,
since Palmer's parents lived in the town, and he doubtless
returned for visits. But most probably they first became
acquainted when Woodward was at home during vacations,
and perhaps attended services at St Margaret's. They became
and remained close friends and, later, collaborators. Plainsong was Palmer's life-long and consuming interest, and
again according to the History he, 'with his unrivalled
knowledge of plainsong and his power of training voices,
which was equalled if not surpassed by his skill as an accom-
panist, soon brought the services to a state of almost perfect
beauty'.[13] Palmer was preparing his widely-used Sarum
Psalter whilst at St Barnabas', together with his Proper
Introits, in addition to the Hymner already mentioned.
Renowned for his learning, and judged to have made a
considerable contribution to the revival of plainsong, the
History relates that he eventually 'became so immersed in the
work of research and editing that he had to give up his work
at St Barnabas'. This was in 1883, a year after Woodward
himself had left Pimlico. Whilst Palmer's first love was for
plainsong, his musical outlook was not unduly narrow and
his policy at St Barnabas' appears to have been to alternate
between plainsong and polyphony. He is said to have introduced Schubert in G as a Mass setting for use at festivals. His
influence on Woodward must have been considerable.

If Palmer encouraged Woodward's interest in plainsong,
then it was probably the second person who encouraged his

interest in hymnody. That person was J. M. Neale, who had
been a friend of Palmer's father during his time in
Cambridge. Woodward, as we have seen, claimed to have
come to know and admire Neale's work whilst he was an
undergraduate, but he cannot have failed to become better
acquainted with that work during his years at St Barnabas'.
Neale, whom Woodward came to venerate and always
referred to as 'my master', was generally regarded as one of
the heroes of the catholic revival in the Church of England, a
position which he had merited both by his immense scholarship and by his role as a Confessor of the Faith. As regards St
Barnabas', he had preached at the church in the octave of its
consecration, and he had collaborated with Thomas
Helmore, who was still connected with the church in
Woodward's time, in producing *Carols for Christmas-tide*
and *Carols for Easter-tide* in 1853 and 1854. Further,
Palmer's *Hymner* contained a good number of Neale's translations of ancient hymns, and Neale and Helmore's own
*Hymnal Noted* was presumably still in use during
Woodward's curacy. Neale had died eight years before
Woodward went to St Barnabas', but his memory would still
have been green, and that not least in the mind of Palmer,
who had known him, through his father, as a boy. Neale,
who had been an extreme Anglo-catholic by the standards of
the time, was – in addition to his learning and his experience
of persecution on account of his teaching and liturgical
practices – a devout and austere priest, besides being a
lover of poetry and music, and it is understandable that
his memory had that same strong appeal for Woodward
as did the Church of St Barnabas' itself. In his later work as
a translator, writer, and compiler of hymns and carols,
and most especially when he himself came to put ancient
Greek hymns into English verse, Woodward would quite
understandably see himself as the successor of Neale, the
one called to continue the work cut short by Neale's early
death. There was nothing either casual or affected about his
calling Neale 'my master', and this admiration, together
maybe with the aspiration to continue Neale's work with
hymnody and carols, must surely have been encouraged,
deepened, and focussed by the years he spent at St Barnabas'.

Whilst we can have a fairly clear picture of the kind of life
which Woodward must have lived during these years, with
carefully organised and disciplined pastoral work amongst
the poor of the parish alternating with what may have been
the more congenial involvement in the daily choral services,
and whilst we can also speculate with some confidence about
the particular influences which may have been working upon
him at this time, there is unfortunately little information
about the more personal aspects of his life during these years.
However five letters written to him by his father survive from
this period, the first dating from 1876, and these are interesting not least in that they give an insight into the happy
relationship which existed between father and son, a relationship which is otherwise suggested only by Woodward's
mention of 'my dearest Father's Gold Watch' in his will. By
this time Woodward's father and step-mother had left
Lancashire for Devon, where they lived at a house called
Glenorleigh in Kingswear, near Dartmouth. Although they
were still living there at the time of the senior Woodward's
death in 1887, he wrote in a letter to his son on December
26th 1878 'My great anxiety now is to sell this beautiful
place, and leave to the next comer the alterations I had
proposed to make ...'. Two years later however he speaks of
wanting to 'finish what I have in hand here', having 'already
very much improved this house', and further says that it is
'looking wonderfully beautiful just now'. The first of the five
letters deserves to be quoted in full: it was written on Boxing
Day 1876, the day before Woodward's birthday.

My dear Georgie,
    One line to wish you may have had a happy Xmas, many
happy returns of tomorrow, and a happy year before you
when it comes in. We are expecting Nellie & Basil tomorrow
and we shall think of you, regretting much that you will be
with us only in thought. It is not the right thing that we all see
so little of each other for there is not much room for many
more meetings if the intervals between them are to be so long.
    I speak from experience that great griefs are felt when
opportunities are so greatly neglected, but then in old times
such things as affections were indulged in and rather cher-
ished. I regret that I can show you so little in a pecuniary way
just now for I am like to be very poor unless Pacific instead of

advancing in Capital advances some dividend. I enclose £5 and next month I hope to send you some more, small though it may be. I don't know that there is much here to interest you. We have had a miserable day of rain with a strong breeze right in & the sea is running high up the rocks. Your Mama obtained a fresh cold by going to Church on Sunday & she has been in the house ever since being unable to attend Xmas services yesterday. The Bidders are quite as nice as ever, of the Heywards we see nothing and almost as little of the Johnstones for a long time. The Jones are away still. I see your Mama is writing to you and she will say her own say.

God bless you my dearest Georgie and give you very many happy years of Peace, Comfort, and happiness.

Your affectionate Father,

G. R. Woodward.

The ordinariness of the letter is appealing: the news of family and neighbours, the weather, worries about how shares are doing, regrets that visits to home are infrequent – it is the kind of letter which innumerable curates have received from their father.

The other letters which Woodward received from his father during these years, and which have survived, are similarly affectionate and domestic. There is further family news; we learn in 1877, for example, that Basil has attracted notice for his sketches, and in 1881 that he is distressed over some 'catastrophe' which has overtaken his fiddle.[14] We hear more of the fortunes of the elder Woodward's stocks and shares, and of his intention to make some kind of financial provision for his son. From these letters, the father emerges as an anxious man, inclined to worry and fret. In 1880 he refers to his 'terror of running short', and besides money he worried too about his wife's health, about the behaviour of his servants, and about the general state of the country. More interesting, we learn too of his disapproval of Catholicism. In a letter written on December 16th 1878 he sent good wishes to Woodward's fellow-curates at St Barnabas', adding that he hopes they are becoming 'more Xtn. and less papistical', whilst in another undated letter which seems to belong to this period he sends regards 'to your fellow monks and I am glad to hear that your Superior (presumably the incumbent) is better'. This undated letter is rather curious; it is headed 'Ye eve of ye fest of Seynt John', and begins 'Rite trustee and well blovd Son'. In it, Woodward's father seems to be parodying the kind of mediaevalism which his son leaned towards, and which was favoured by certain of the adherents of the catholic revival in the Church of England. After writing in this vein for some lines, he continued:

> And is this the sort of rubbishy style we in the 19th century with telephones, telegraphs, telescopes etc. are to be brought back to; only 400 years since all this rubbish has been shot into the dustbin of Eternity and a few poor benighted idiots wish to restore it. It cannot be, progress will be made all the more rapidly, because of the contrast between true light and obsolete darkness ... alas it is not pleasant in these days to hear of pilgrimages, bone worship, picture worship, of winking Virgins, I have no doubt, plenty of them in every large town and are we to be brought back to our Lady of Walsingham, St Thomas à Becket and all such, that these sinners are to intercede for us sinners? The days of <u>Priestcraft</u> are nearly over, and true goodness will have its day yet. But I ought not to bother you on your birthday with these remarks, only I thought that you might look inward on such a day, and calmly ask if there is need of such addition to our Holy Testament.

Clearly Woodward did not derive his Anglo-catholicism from his father, whose religious opinions, otherwise rarely expressed in the surviving letters, he must have considered very unenlightened. The sentiments of the letter are somewhat ironic in view of both the archaic literary style which Woodward later adopted for his carol-writing, and of the devotion to Our Lady of Walsingham which he apparently embraced in the last years of his life.

The letter written in 1877, like that which survives from the previous year, has an enclosure of five pounds, but this time with the admonition that the money is ...

> For your <u>own</u> bodily comfort, the sustenance of your thought, or the amusement of your mind, and not to be replaced out of your own funds for other purposes. See what a child I take you still to be when I cannot trust you with one hundred shillings without making stipulations, that it is not to go to canting old women who say they are dying and would rob you of your own dinner to stuff their old carceses [sic] withal.

Ten pounds was sent the following year, this time to enable Woodward to pay some small bill, and with the request that he should 'put the balance into your stomach or on to your back'. It must have been easy for a priest in a parish like St Barnabas' to have used his available resources to help the victims of poverty which he would have seen daily, but this was something which did not meet with the approval of Woodward's father. Nor, it seems, did some plan which Woodward advanced for sending a needy Pimlico boy down to Devon; in the same letter of 1878 he wrote 'I am sure that if you cannot manage the boy you proposed to send us, I am quite sure we could not, and anything connected with Dartmouth is quite out of the question. Lower and lower sink these people in my estimation'. Father and son did not apparently see eye to eye on everything.

Woodward spent eight years at St Barnabas', during which time he worked under three incumbents. Bagshawe, who came from All Saints, Margaret Street, in 1876 to replace White, was remembered for having introduced eucharistic vestments at St Barnabas', for having written a controversial book entitled *The Priest in Absolution*, and for having been Master of the Society of the Holy Cross. He retired through ill-health in 1879, and was succeeded by The Revd. Alfred Gurney, who was to remain in office until 1898. For Woodward, these eight years must have been both stimulating and formative. Liturgically, musically, spiritually and intellectually St Barnabas' was a stimulating place to be at that time, and it seems that the people, principles, and practices which he came to know there played a large part in moulding him. Two of his predecessors as assistant curates had left Pimlico to work in Norfolk: The Revd Henry Langston Rumsey had become Vicar of St John Maddermarket, Norwich, in 1872, and The Revd Edmund Worlledge, Vicar of Wood Dalling in 1879. In 1882 Woodward too was offered a parish in Norfolk, that of Little Walsingham with Houghton St Giles'. He accepted, and left the noise and excitement of London for what was then a remote and intensely rural part of East Anglia.

# CHAPTER THREE

# WALSINGHAM 1882–1888

Woodward was thirty-four when he became Vicar of Little
Walsingham with Houghton-in-the Dale in the diocese of
Norwich.[1] Walsingham, a village of moderate size but of
unusual charm, is set in a particularly attractive part of
North Norfolk, about five miles inland from the sea. Lying in
the shallow valley of the River Stiffkey, it is a village of
considerable interest both historically and architecturally.
Historically, because in the mediaeval period it was a
renowned centre of pilgrimage, ranking in England only
second to Canterbury. The Blessed Virgin Mary is reputed to
have appeared to Richeldis de Faverches, Lady of the Manor,
in 1061 and the Shrine which Richeldis established at Mary's
command, based upon a replica of the Holy House at
Nazareth, drew great crowds of pilgrims. These included
every English monarch from Edward I to Henry VIII, the
latter changing in the course of his reign from devout pilgrim
to greedy despoiler.[2]

Architecturally, the vestiges of Walsingham's past status
remain. The remnants of the priory of Augustinian Canons
which administered the Shrine include an impressive gate-
house and refectory together with the east end of the priory
church, whilst the country house known as The Abbey,
which lies just back from the High Street, has at its core the
mediaeval Prior's Lodging. On the edge of the village stand
what are considered to be the most complete remains of a
Franciscan friary in the country, and the High Street and
Common Place are lined with timber-framed houses dating
mainly from the fifteenth-century, some of which were originally built as pilgrim hostels.

In the late sixteen-thirties, the remains of the Priory,
together with much of the village and all of the surrounding
farmland, was purchased by John Warner, Bishop of
Rochester (1581–1666). He bequeathed the estate to his
nephew and Archdeacon, John Lee, and so founded the Lee
Warner family, which remained in possession of it until the

second decade of the present century.[3] With the estate went
the patronage of the living. The squire who appointed
Woodward as Vicar was Henry James Lee Warner
(1809–1886), who had succeeded his father, Daniel Henry
Lee Warner, in 1858. He was married to Ellen Rosetta
Bullock (1824–1910), and he had a brother, Septimus Lee
Warner, who held the living from 1860 until his death at the
age of forty-one in 1870. Septimus was the third member of
the family in succession to be appointed; James Lee Warner
had been Vicar from 1807 until 1834, and an earlier Henry
James Lee Warner from 1834 to 1859. The latter, Canon
Lee Warner, had built the square late-Georgian-style
Vicarage in 1845, and it was into this house, surrounded by
a meadow running down to the River Stiffkey and situated
on the edge of the village, that Woodward moved in 1882.
It was a spacious but by the standards of the day not
excessively large house. South of it, across the Norwich
Road, lay the walled grounds of the Abbey, whilst the
parish church was reached by means of a road which had
been sunk a few feet below ground level as part of the land-
scaping of the Abbey park carried out in the early years of
the nineteenth-century.

Woodward's appointment to the living of Walsingham is
difficult to account for. He had, after all, spent eight years as
curate at one of the most notoriously extreme Anglo-catholic
churches in London, and had never before lived in a rural
community. In his book *Walsingham Way* Colin Stephenson
tried to explain the appointment by saying that Henry James
Lee Warner and his wife had become 'ardent Puseyites', and
that having employed the architect G. E. Street (1824–1881)
to restore the parish church in accordance with the principles
of the Cambridge Camden Society, they then 'produced Fr
Woodward to introduce the right sort of religion to go with
it'.[4] But this is unconvincing. Family tradition certainly held
that Henry James had been 'rather high church', but no more
than that. And whilst in G. E. Street he had indeed employed
a high church architect to restore his church, this had taken
place in 1866, since when Henry James had appointed new
incumbents both in 1870 and 1871, neither of whom had
been of an Anglo-catholic persuasion. Further, Stephenson

asserts that Woodward was a relation of the Lee Warners, on the grounds that Henry James' grandfather, Daniel Henry, had borne the name Woodward before he inherited the Walsingham estate from a cousin of his mother, the eccentric Henry Lee Warner, in 1804, and, in accordance with Henry Lee Warner's will, had changed his name and arms to those of Lee Warner.[5] But there is no evidence at all for saying that Woodward was a relative; the fact that he bore the same surname as that originally borne by Henry James Lee Warner's grandfather seems to have been purely coincidental. Henry James' grandfather had originated in Bristol, with certain lands in Gloucestershire, and even the possibility of these Woodwards being connected with the Worcestershire Woodwards to whom G. R. Woodward claimed distant relationship, is uncertain.

How Woodward came to be offered the living remains a mystery, but it is tempting to make one speculation. This is that Woodward's name may perhaps have been suggested to Henry James Lee Warner by a fellow high-churchman and member of the Norfolk gentry, the scholarly and cosmopolitan W. J. Birkbeck (1859–1916). At that time Birkbeck was living just outside Norwich at Thorpe St Andrew; he moved to Stratton Strawless Hall in 1901. Certainly Birkbeck was deeply interested in plainsong, visiting the great centres of the plainsong revival, Solesmes in France and Maredsous in Belgium in the 1880s, and it is inconceivable that he was not familiar with St Barnabas' Pimlico at this time in view of its reputation for the performance of plainsong. He was certainly interested in its affairs in the following decade, when he wrote to Lord Halifax concerning the appointment of a new incumbent,[6] but his interest may stretch back well before this, and if so he must almost certainly have been acquainted with Woodward. The greater uncertainty is whether or not Birkbeck knew Lee Warner – or perhaps his son, Henry (both Henry and Birkbeck were keen amateur 'cellists) – and had the opportunity to advise on the appointment to the living. We do not know.

Woodward's immediate predecessor at Walsingham was the Revd William Martin, and in April 1880, two years

before his eleven-year incumbency came to an end, he
acquired a new Preachers' Book.[7] In this, Sunday by Sunday,
he recorded preacher and text, and since the scope of the
book was wider than the title might suggest, he also noted
details of the Sunday collection, the date and time of
funerals, and the number of communicants at the fortnightly
celebration of the Holy Communion – on average around
twenty-five. On September 24th 1882, after recording that
the silver collection money amounted to two shillings and
nine pence and the copper to seven shillings and three half-
pence, the scrawling and somewhat indolent hand of Mr.
Martin comes to an end, to be replaced on Sunday October
1st by the small, neat, and purposeful writing of the new
incumbent, George Ratcliffe Woodward. Woodward records
that the Holy Communion was celebrated at 8.00 am on that
day, with thirty-seven people receiving the Sacrament. At
11.00 am he read Mattins, the Litany, and – as a new incumbent was required to do – he also read the Thirty Nine
Articles of Religion. He preached on the text 'I am the Good
Shepherd; the good shepherd lays down his life for the sheep'
(John 10:11). On the following Sunday, October 8th, there
was another celebration of the Holy Communion, this
time following immediately after 11.00 am Mattins, with
the impressive number of fifty-four communicants. However Evensong that day, according to the local newspaper,
'attracted a congregation of almost unprecedented character,
the church being crowded in every part even when standing
room only could be obtained. The number was estimated at
over 800 persons, the church having but little over 500
sittings'.[8] People were presumably moved by curiosity
regarding their new Vicar, who by now had spent a week in
the parish and who cannot have failed to attract attention
through his tall athletic figure – James Horsfall recalled that
he was six foot one tall, and strongly built – his striking good
looks, and perhaps above all through the kind of clerical
dress which he wore, and which can never before, one
imagines, have been seen in North Norfolk. The few
photographs which survive from this period all show him
wearing the soutane, usually topped by a wide-brimmed
clerical hat, and it seems that this was his normal dress until

the end of his life. The extraordinarily large congregation on that occasion may also have been moved by curiosity regarding the celebration of Harvest Festival, which at that time was still relatively novel, and seems to have been kept at Walsingham for the first time on this Sunday.[9]

At the very beginning of his ministry in this Norfolk village Woodward had established a weekly celebration of the Holy Communion on Sundays, and shortly afterwards he began additional celebrations on certain weekdays, having, of course, been used to a daily celebration during his years at St Barnabas'. First the feast of St Luke was kept, with six communicants, and soon afterwards the feast of All Saints was marked by a celebration at 8.00 am, at which there were eighteen communicants, Woodward being the celebrant; at 9.00 am there was a further celebration by G. H. Palmer, who happened to be staying at the Vicarage. All Souls Day saw a further celebration, and thus the pattern was set. By late November a proper Service Register had been procured, and Mr Martin's Preachers' Book, although only one-quarter full, was laid aside. What had been indicated in that book was the fact that there had been more than just a change of incumbent at Walsingham; there had been a change in the religious tradition. More precisely, the effects of the Catholic revival begun fifty years previously in Oxford, with its emphasis on the centrality of eucharistic worship and the sacramental life, had begun to be felt in this far corner of East Anglia, as in so many other places, rural as well as urban. Soon the presentation of worship, the furniture and the vesture, would begin to change, just as the pattern of services had changed, whilst a shift in teaching is suggested by the fact that before long the parish was asked to support the new Anglo-catholic societies such as the English Church Union, the Guild of All Souls, and the Confraternity of the Blessed Sacrament, Woodward becoming a member of the latter in the year he went to Walsingham.[10]

There is no record of just what ceremonial, furnishings, and vesture Woodward may have introduced at Walsingham,[11] but there is a most detailed record of the changes which occurred at his other church, a mile away at Houghton-in-the Dale (now more usually called Houghton St Giles').

Just as Little Walsingham Church had been restored in 1866 by G. E. Street, at the instigation of Henry James Lee Warner, so too St Giles' Church had been rebuilt – with rather more sensitivity – by another distinguished architect, W. Eden Nesfield, in 1879. The year after his arrival in Walsingham, Woodward appointed a Curate-in-Charge to live in Houghton; he was the Revd Edward Fenton Elwin, son of the renowned Vicar of Booton, and he kept a remarkable Log Book in which he recorded not only parish events but also his liturgical and other innovations.[12] We learn for example that eucharistic vestments were worn for the first time on February 18th 1883; that a server first assisted at the Holy Communion on February 24th, and that Altar Lights made their appearance on March 25th of that year. That a daily celebration of the Holy Communion was finally established on April 10th 1887; that wafer bread began to be used in November, and that a processional cross came into use the following year. These things were clearly done with Woodward's approval, for whilst he seems to have given Elwin a fairly free hand in running Houghton, he, Woodward, remained the incumbent and in overall charge. The usages which he allowed at Houghton he most probably introduced himself at Walsingham, and the Patron, having brought him from St Barnabas' Pimlico can hardly have expected any less. Not of course that the liturgical practices in even 'advanced' parishes in the eighteen-eighties would have been particularly 'extreme' by the standards of, say, the nineteen-twenties; at St Barnabas' itself, for example, incense was not introduced until 1894, nor perpetual reservation of the Blessed Sacrament until 1901.[13] Did Woodward's changes in the worship at Walsingham meet with opposition? The only suggestion that they did is contained in a 'funeral tribute' which appeared in *The Eastern Daily Press* on March 9th 1934, a few days after his death. In referring to Woodward's work at Walsingham, the so-far unidentified writer, one 'V.N.G.' wrote that 'In restoring the dignity of public worship to what it is today, the standard of most cathedrals, he endured considerable opposition'. But since there is no contemporary (or other) corroboration for this, and in view of the fact that it was written half a century after the events in question, it should probably be treated with caution.

In his Log Book Elwin also gives details of the musical developments at Houghton-in-the-Dale, and these probably give some indication of the pattern of church music which Woodward was encouraging in Walsingham. We read of the first choir practice at Houghton having been held on February 23rd 1883, and that the choir was provided with cassocks and surplices in the September of the year. A month later Elwin records that 'Doran and Nottingham's Psalter is now used, & Evensong on Weekdays is now Sung instead of Said, excepting the Psalms'. This book would have been *A Choir Directory of Plain Song* by J. W. Doran and S. Nottingham, which was published in 1879. If, extraordinary as it now seems, the small church at Houghton, which served a mere hamlet, had a daily sung Evensong, then it is not surprising that Walsingham Parish Church, serving a much larger community and with an incumbent used to daily choral services, should have had the same. In fact Doran and Nottingham's *Choir Directory* clearly was used at Walsingham too, for a copy survives in the parish records inscribed 'Henry Lee Warner from G. R. Woodward. December 15th 1882'.[14] This dates from just a few weeks after Woodward's arrival in the parish, and suggests that the new incumbent was seeking from the start to involve his patron – or more probably his son, Henry, who was Woodward's senior by just one year – in what was taking place in the musical life of the parish church. Notation is provided at the back of the book for the Versicles and Responses at Morning and Evening Prayer, and there in a neat hand which is presumably Lee Warner's is written 'Ist time Eve of Epiphany. 1883.' Further on, against the Litany set to plainsong is noted 'Novr. 1882': in view of the date of the inscription, Lee Warner may have been recording here what had already taken place, and if this is the case it suggests that Woodward had begun the use of plainsong within just a few weeks of his induction. There is one further entry in the Houghton Log Book which is of interest as regards the musical life of the parish: on September 7th 1887, the Wednesday within the Octave of the Feast of St Giles, Elwin notes against 7.30 pm Evensong

'Some of the men from Walsingham Choir came over and assisted, and the Revd G. R. Woodward accompanied the singing with the Euphonium'. Dom Anslem Hughes, after refering to weekday choral evensongs at Walsingham during Woodward's incumbency – from which it seems certain that he did indeed introduce daily choral services – wrote 'later, his most famous instrument was the euphonium, which he delighted to play in procession. I believe, but am not sure, that this performance took place at St Barnabas', Pimlico'.[15] Hughes seems to be refering to Woodward's second spell at St Barnabas', 1894–1898, but clearly he was playing the euphonium some years before this, and indeed one of the few photographs of him to survive shows him playing the instrument outside the front door of Walsingham Vicarage. Not, however, that the use of the euphonium was restricted to accompanying worship: on at least one occasion he played it at a village concert at Walsingham, the audience finding it 'exceedingly effective' and according to the report in the local newspaper, they loudly demanded encores.[16]

Woodward's first sermon had been preached on the Good Shepherd, and there seems reason to believe that he was as diligent in his pastoral activities as in his musical and liturgical ones, involving himself with the people and events of the village from the start. Thus on his first All Saints Day, a month or so after his arrival – when he and Palmer had both celebrated the Holy Communion in the morning – it was reported in the *Lynn Advertiser* under the heading 'A Good Example' that ...

> ... the aged poor of the almshouses, some twenty in number, were invited to a substantial dinner at the Abbey Gate Coffee House by the new Vicar, the Revd G. R. Woodward. Several ladies from The Abbey (including Mrs Lee Warner) volunteered their services as waiters and in the afternoon amused the old people with singing and music. The arrangements of the coffee house officials gave every satisfaction and the recipients expressed themselves in terms of profound gratitude at the kindness of their generous entertainers.[17]

Later it was reported in the same paper that the Vicar had given his 'annual' Christmas gift to the almshouse dwellers, of tea and two shillings and sixpence each. On another occasion it was the children of the Church Sunday School who benefited; eighty of them, according to the newspaper,

> ... enjoying a capital treat through the kindness of the Revd G. R. Woodward, Mrs and Misses Lee Warner of Hindringham, and other friends. After a short service at church, the children, accompanied by their teachers, proceeded to the school rooms, where a very bountiful tea awaited them. Games were then indulged in whilst the teachers partook of refreshment, and the whole party then proceeded to the Abbey Gate Coffee House, in the large room of which was provided an entertainment consisting of a 'Charade' (discovered to mean 'Walsingham') and 'Tableaux Vivant'. The latter, representing the well known tales of 'Cinderella' and 'The Sleeping Beauty' were exceedingly pretty and much delighted the youthful audience ...[18]

That same year there was also a Summer Treat for the children; again there was a short service, after which they 'proceeded to the Parsonage grounds, where swings, racing, and games of all description were indulged in. About 4.00 pm they sat down to a bountiful tea. A quantity of prizes, presents, and toys were then distributed among the children, after which games were continued until dark when the youngsters left the ground'.[19]

On yet another occasion it was the Church Bells Ringers who received Woodward's hospitality. Again the newspaper account is worth quoting, since it succeeds in giving something of the flavour of the occasion:

> On Wednesday evening the bell ringers were generously entertained to supper by the Vicar, the Revd G. R. Woodward, at the Bull Inn. The Churchwardens of the Parish were also included in the invitation. A substantial meal was tastefully put upon the table by host Ives. The Vicar presided ... The cloth being removed the Chairman expressed himself as greatly pleased to see around him those whom he was proud to call his friends, and expatiated at some length on the duties of church bell ringers. A conversation then took place as to the condition of the bell tower and the necessity of the bells being rehung, as in their present condition the ringers could not do justice to the fine old peal ... The ringers having their handbells in the room played at intervals some very pretty peals. The health of the Vicar, the Churchwardens, and the Ringers were drunk in the course of the evening, and at the departure of the guests all expressed their thanks to the Vicar.[20]

Hospitable, sociable, but serious in explaining the duties of church bell ringers, this is an attractive picture of Woodward. And it is interesting to see his enthusiasm for bell-ringing in view of the fact that bells would feature so frequently in the carols he would write in later years, most memorably in his best-known carol 'Ding Dong! Merrily on High'.[21] Maybe this enthusiasm had first been kindled at St Barnabas', which Bennett had equipped with a fine ring. The impression given here and elsewhere is that Woodward was a popular parish priest, lively, generous, and imaginative, as well as being devout and earnest. Yet another newspaper report, having given details of the well-attended Easter services in 1884, concluded 'It is all but needless to say that these results are mainly due to the ever zealous and untiring labours of the hard working Vicar ... and it is hoped that people will continue to support a minister so devoted to the work of his church and his parish.'[22]

But hardworking though he was, it seems that Woodward still found time to enjoy his hobbies and his friends. Amongst the former was Beekeeping, an interest which he may have inherited from his father, who remarked in a letter written on April 9th 1883 that he had 'now only two hives of Bees left'. Most probably, however, it was at Walsingham that Woodward first acquired hives of his own, and he may have benefited from the enthusiasm and expertise of one of his parishioners, a local bee-keeper called Mr R. J. Bayes, who was son of the village surgeon. The *Lynn Advertiser* reported on September 1st 1883 that Woodward had recently taken the chair at a lecture given by Bayes called 'How to make money from Bees', whilst four years later Elwin records in his Log Book that Woodward himself had given a lecture to the Band of Mercy at Houghton on 'Modern Bee-Keeping'. Bees, like bells, would often appear in his future verses, perhaps most curiously in a translation from the Greek in which St Basil is likened to a bee:

> 'Hail! work-bee in the church of Christ,
>     Saint Basil, blessed in the high'st!
> For thou with sting of heav'nly zeal
>     Did's't arm thyself, and didest deal
> A deadly wound to blasphemies
>     Of God-detested heresies.'[23]

Of the friends he saw during this period of his life, G. H. Palmer has already been mentioned: his several appearances in the Service Register at Walsingham suggest that he made various visits, and it seems likely that the man who has been called 'the most learned of English plainsong experts'[24] would have been asked to advise on the plainsong used at the daily services in the parish church. Another occasional visitor from London was Fr Stanton, the almost legendary Assistant Priest at St Alban's Holborn, the *Lynn Advertiser* reporting on October 18th 1884 that he had preached twice at Walsingham on the previous Sunday in support of his seaside home for postmen at St Leonard's-on-Sea. Palmer and Stanton were together at Walsingham for Woodward's last Harvest Festival, in October 1888, and the newspaper account of the occasion deserves to be quoted, not least for the details which it gives about the pattern of worship:

> On Sunday the parish church was the scene of bright and joyous thanksgiving services. It was very chastely decorated with flowers and corn; the font, pulpit, chancel screen and communion table being particularly beautiful ... The Holy Communion (choral) was celebrated at 8.00 am. There were over 40 communicants. The Revd G. R. Woodward was the celebrant, the Revd G. H. Palmer assisting. At 11.00 am matins and litany were sung, followed by a powerful sermon by the Revd A. H. Stanton M.A. of St Alban's, London ... at 3.00 pm the usual catechising service was held, and at 6.30 pm choral evensong, at which Mr Stanton again preached. The church was filled to overflowing, and it was estimated that over 700 persons were present ... The anthem at the evening service, "O taste and see" was exceedingly well rendered by a full choir, with orchestral accompaniments, and the Hallelujah chorus closed the services for the day.'[25]

Members of Woodward's family also came to stay at the Vicarage; his father concludes a letter written on September 30th 1885 by saying 'My respect and love to your good ladies and warm remembrances to the Abbey and its inhabitants also the good folks of the village, who Basil tells me speak still warmly of me'. The 'good ladies' referred to are probably the Misses Walter, who seem to have assisted Woodward in his various works, and whose address is given as The Vicarage both during and immediately after his incumbency; possibly they were older unmarried ladies who lived at Vicarage Cottage. In another letter, of March 14th 1887, the senior Woodward writes 'Give my best love to the Miss Walters and to Alice but I cannot promise that I shall be able to walk any more with them, for my locomotive powers are as crippled as my hands are ...' His sister Nellie was also a visitor, and she was reported in the *Lynn Advertiser* to have attended a village entertainment in 1883 at which she both played the piano and won first prize in a spelling bee.[26] As regards friends close at hand, presumably Elwin, with his similar religious and musical interests, was more than just a colleague, and perhaps W. J. Birkbeck was a visitor at the Vicarage. Like Woodward, he was an enthusiastic classicist, reading Greek for pleasure, and according to Lord Halifax he was 'an accomplished musician, playing the organ with infinite skill and taste, and he was expert in all matters connected with hymnology'.[27] Birkbeck was also like Woodward in being an amateur 'cellist; Hughes claiming that the latter gave 'cello recitals after the daily choral even-song at Walsingham.[28] Later the two men collaborated on a translation of the Greek *Acathist Hymn*, published in 1917, a year after Birkbeck's death, but they may well have known each other during Woodward's years in Norfolk, and in view of Birkbeck's study of the contemporary revival of plainsong on the Continent there would have been various matters of common interest.

Also amongst Woodward's friends and associates at this time were the Mrs and Misses Lee Warner of Hindringham, who had assisted him with the Church Sunday School Party. Mrs Lee Warner, born Jane Hopkins of Tidmarsh House, Berkshire, was the widow of the Revd Septimus Lee Warner, brother of Squire Henry James Lee Warner of Walsingham Abbey. Septimus, born 1819 and ten years younger than his brother, had been the first of the four clergymen whom Henry James presented to the living of Walsingham in the course of his long life. Septimus succeeded his cousin Canon James Lee Warner in 1860, dying ten years later at the age of forty-one, after which his widow and their six children, a son, Chandos, and five daughters, Alice Dorothy, Alexandra, Emily, Joan, and Annie, moved to a house just outside the nearby village of Hindringham.[29] This mid-nineteenth-century house, which was not unlike the Vicarage they had vacated in size and appearance, was built on an ancient site and was formerly known as Godfrey's Hall. It seems to have been re-named Lohengrin Lodge at this time, suggesting that the Septimus Lee Warners shared in the contemporary enthusiasm for Wagner's music, as indeed did Woodward himself. During these years there seem to have been frequent 'Entertainments' at the Abbey Gate Coffee House in Walsingham, consisting of a mixture of tableaux vivants, songs, music for piano and other instruments, scenes from plays, and recitations. The Misses Lee Warner appear to have taken a leading part in these, especially Alexandra, who played the piano. One of these entertainments, in February 1884, was reported to have been 'under the direction and management of the Revd G. R. Woodward', and on that occasion Elwin read from Mark Twain, whilst Alexandra and Woodward played together, she the piano and he the euphonium. It was reported that this entertainment had given 'great satisfaction'.[30] It was not surprising that Woodward should have been attracted to this clerical and musical family, nor that they in turn should have been attracted to him, a handsome, relatively young, and well-educated bachelor of independent means, and in due time he became engaged to the eldest of the sisters, Alice Dorothy Lee Warner, who may well be the Alice whom the senior Woodward spoke of walking with in one of his letters. The marriage took place in 1889, a few months after Woodward had left Walsingham.

The letters which Woodward's father wrote to him during his years at Walsingham – of which nine survive – indicate that the father continued to fret about business and financial matters, although it is difficult to construct any overall picture of his affairs from the various disconnected pieces of information which the letters supply. He seems to have been involved in a somewhat acrimonious dispute with another member of the family, writing in 1884 'not for anything would I allow that I was put out of the way by the doings of your precious cousin, that would be his greatest triumph', but the nature of the dispute and the identity of the cousin are both unclear. In the following year he wrote 'I wish particularly to know if you are in dire need of some money. In June I did not owe more than £50 in all, now I am in double that amount and when I go I hope not to owe 1/- but let me know all about your wants for I have money in the Bank enough thank God ...' The letters contain family news – Mama's health and not having heard from Basil being recurring themes, and also he writes in 1883 – from Hooton in Cheshire, where he had been staying whilst attending to business matters in Liverpool – about Nellie's engagement, saying that he is 'extremely thankful to think that Dear Nellie was about to fall in the hands of a <u>gentleman</u> and not be thrown away upon anyone who would not or could not appreciate her many qualities', adding 'if she should prove to be one tenth <u>part as good as her Mother</u>, she will still be a treasure in any man's house'.

Woodward was also sent news of the house and garden at Kingswear: there is reference to the 'new building', 'dedicated to you as an Oratory and to Basil as a smoking sanctuary', and complaints about the damage done by rabbits to the plants in the garden, amongst the victims being pansies which had been sent in boxes from Walsingham, together with bulbs, in August 1883. Only on one occasion in the surviving letters did the father show his continuing anti-Catholic feelings, when he stipulates that some money he had sent must not be 'spent in wax candles and such rubbish', and hopes that the devil may 'take away the Pope and all papists'. His deteriorating health is apparent in his handwriting and verbal expression, besides being explicitly referred to, as in May 1884 when he writes 'I am getting past work and there will be a muddle of work for some one to put in order some day'.

Since Woodward is best remembered as a writer and composer of carols, it is interesting to find that he was already involved with this kind of music during his time at Walsingham, certainly by way of performance. There is a newspaper account of Easter in the village which records that 'In the early hours of the morning the choir boys sang Easter carols through the town', whilst in church there was 'catechising and carols' at 3.00 pm.[31] Again at the Sunday School treat in January 1884 there were 'several Christmas carols sung by the children' according to the local newspaper. But already Woodward seems to have been interested in more than just the performance of carols. Writing to the widow of his friend Charles Wood some forty years later, in 1926, he recalled that the Latin words to the mediaeval carol 'Angelus ad Virginem' had been 'copied out by G. H. Palmer and sent to me when I was at Walsingham, in or about 1883',[32] an indication that he may well have been involved in the translation even if not in the composition of carols at this early date.

The six years which Woodward spent at Walsingham seem to have been a particularly happy period in his life, and that from the start: replying to a letter written just a few months after he went there, his father began 'I was very glad to hear from you again, and that you were meeting so much kindness and like the country so well'. It was a time when he was engaged in congenial pursuits in a very pleasant surroundings, seeing friends, making music, and being on equally good terms with both the occupants of the almshouses and of the Abbey. A time, too, when he became engaged to be married to someone who seems to have shared his interests. These were also years when he had the satisfaction of propagating the Anglo-catholic teaching and worship which he had experienced at St Barnabas' and which he had embraced with such conviction, taking these things as a missionary or evangelist out from the metropolis to a place where the like had not been known for more than three centuries. He seems to have looked back on these years with something akin to nostalgia, still describing himself on title-pages as 'Sometime Vicar of Walsingham' forty years later.

Woodward accepted the offer of the Rectory of Chelmondiston, a village near Ipswich in the neighbouring county of Suffolk, at the end of 1888. At his last Sunday School Christmas treat, on Friday December 28th, he presented each teacher with a book as a parting gift, and on the following Sunday he conducted his last services at Walsingham. The local newspaper reported that:

The Revd gentleman has spent upward of six years in this place, during which time he has always endeared himself to a large majority of his congregation. On the evening of Sunday the church was crowded, it being understood that at that service Mr Woodward would bid his parishioners farewell ... His discourse was listened to throughout with marked attention, and many of the congregation were visibly affected. A substantial mark of the respect and esteem in which he is held will shortly be presented to him.[33]

The 'substantial mark of respect and esteem' took the form of a sum of money, given together with a neatly written-out list of the subscribers. The list, which is headed by Mrs Lee Warner, widow of Woodward's patron, and her son – both of whom contributed one pound – also contains many subscriptions of one or two shillings from poorer parishioners, together with the sum of three shillings and sixpence collected by the 'Abbey Servants'.

# CHAPTER FOUR

# CHELMONDISTON 1888–1894

It is easy to see why Woodward went to Harrow, to Cambridge, and to Pimlico: family connections, the availability of a scholarship, and his particular liturgical and musical tastes – these, respectively, adequately explain each of the moves. By contrast, the reason why he went to Walsingham is unclear and so too is his reason for leaving the parish after just six years. By nineteenth-century standards it was a short incumbency, and his forthcoming marriage into the Lee Warner family might have been expected to root him more firmly in North Norfolk life. Colin Stephenson suggests that it was his marriage which brought the move about. He writes 'in one way Fr Woodward was a disappointment for he got married, and the Lee Warners were very much in favour of clerical celibacy. From that time they would never again speak of him as "Father", but always "Mr Woodward", which is probably why he only stayed six years.'[1] But this is again unconvincing. Henry James Lee Warner, who Stephenson called an 'ardent Puseyite', had in fact died in 1886, two years before Woodward left Walsingham, and had been succeeded by his son Henry who was apparently both mildly eccentric and not 'ardent' in religious matters, and who was quite happy to travel down to London to attend the Woodward wedding in 1889. Besides which Henry James had appointed a married priest in 1871, Mr Martin, and at this time it was only in the most extreme Anglo-catholic circles that clerical marriage was frowned upon. Most adherents of the movement had no difficulties in this matter, and of the four heroes of the revival who preached at St Barnabas' in the octave of its consecration, Keble, Pusey, Manning, and Neale, each one had been a married priest. It is most unlikely that Henry Lee Warner, although unmarried himself, held strong views on this matter (nor, furthermore, is it likely that the Lee Warners would ever have called their Vicar 'Father' at this date.)

There may of course have been personal reasons, now unknown, for Woodward's move to Suffolk in 1888, but it is probably fruitless to speculate on these. Most likely it was his continuing and deepening interest in carols and plainsong which made him wish to be nearer London in order to meet and consult with other enthusiasts, and to be closer to the books and manuscripts in the British Museum which would occupy so much of his attention during the next few decades. Certainly interest in the study and revival of plainsong was burgeoning at this time, and just a few days before Woodward left Walsingham – he was instituted at Chelmondiston on December 6th 1888 – seven men met in London to form the Plainsong and Mediaeval Music Society, on whose Council he would serve for twenty-eight years. These men included Athelstan Riley – who is said to have introduced W. J. Birkbeck to Anglo-catholicism at Eton – whilst Birkbeck and Woodward were amongst the earliest members. They must, therefore, have come into contact with each other at this time, even if not before. Walter Howard Frere (1863–1938), a notable scholar and later Bishop of Truro, joined the Society in 1891, and three years later he was contributing harmonisations to one of Woodward's early collections of carols. It was not until 1904 however that Woodward became a member of the council of the Society, and so the move to Chelmondiston cannot have been prompted specifically by duties in this direction – quite apart from the fact that the decision to move must have been made before the Society was actually formed.[2]

If Woodward's wish to be within easier reach of London is understandable, then why in particular did he accept the offer of Chelmondiston, near Ipswich, a place which, whilst it is certainly considerably closer to the capital than Walsingham, is not exactly in the city or home counties? And how, for that matter, did he come to be offered the living in the first place? The patron of the living does not seem to offer any clue (it was the Lord Chancellor) but there is a certain connection with that part of Suffolk which may have been significant. When in 1898 Woodward published a book entitled *Legends of the Saints* it was dedicated to Frances Mary Skinner, and two years later he preached a sermon at St

Barnabas', subsequently published, to mark her death. In that sermon he described her as 'the friend of Dr Pusey, Dean Church, Mr Bennett, and many other of the old Tractarians, [who] has been for nearly fifty years a constant worshipper at St Barnabas'.[3] She had, therefore, known Woodward during the eight years of his first curacy, and it so happens that her country home was The Chantry, Ipswich, just five miles from Chelmondiston. Further, when Woodward's *The Seven Sleepers of Ephesus* appeared in 1902 it was dedicated to Lady Kathleen Skinner and Edgar Louis Skinner. Lady Kathleen, who was married to Frances Mary's son Charles Lancelot Andrewes Skinner, was a daughter of the Revd The Hon. W. W. B. Ponsonby, who was Rector of Stutton in Suffolk from 1884 until 1894 before succeeding his brother as 7th Earl of Bessborough in 1895. Stutton is only three or four miles from Chelmondiston, and coincidentally a place with which the Lee Warners were connected through their relatives-by-marriage the Parry Okedens. It is possible that Woodward's friendship with the Skinner family may have played a part in his being offered and accepting the living of Chelmondiston.

His new parish was set in a particularly attractive part of Suffolk, on the peninsula between the estuaries of the Orwell and the Stour. Chelmondiston village lies about half a mile above the former river, and is joined to it by a short valley in which the brick-built Rectory, since demolished, was situated. The village was smaller than Walsingham, but was like it in that it belonged to a single estate – in this case the Woolverstone estate, owned by Capt. Hugh Berners RN (1801–1891) of Woolverstone Hall, the house and its extensive park lying just to the west of the village. The church, which was destroyed by a flying bomb in 1944 (just as Woodward's other church, Little Walsingham, was destroyed by fire in 1961) was generally smaller and less distinguished than the church at Walsingham. A low building without a clerestory or south aisle it had been virtually rebuilt in 1864. During Woodward's incumbency further work took place: in 1891 the Chancel was reconstructed under the direction of the architect George Frederick Bodley (1827–1907), who was described by his fellow architect Norman Shaw in that same year as the man 'whom many consider our greatest architect'.[4] When Capt. Berners had re-built Woolverstone Church two years earlier he had used the more pedestrian west-country architect James Piers St Aubyn (1815–1895). Berners and his executors largely financed the work at Chelmondiston in 1891, but the choice of architect was almost certainly that of Woodward. Bodley had been carrying out various pieces of work at St Barnabas' Pimlico since 1887, and it is easy to imagine that having seen and admired his work there, Woodward would wish to use him on his own church.

The work done at Chelmondiston was of just the sort that one would expect from an Anglo-catholic architect working with an Anglo-catholic incumbent in this period. The Chancel, Chancel arch, and Vestry – described in the Faculty for the work as being 'inconvenient and in a bad state of repair' – were all rebuilt, the former being given a ceiling painted by W. D. Powell of Lincoln and hangings by Watts and Co. of London. A new High Altar and gradine were supplied, together with new choir stalls and communion rails, and there was a re-arrangement of the seating in the Nave.[5] Woodward's involvement in the part-rebuilding and re-furnishing at Chelmondiston is interesting because apart from this there is comparatively little evidence for any interest he may have had in the visual arts, although such an interest might also be suggested by the fact that during his first curacy at St Barnabas' he possessed a book on ancient monumental brasses – a book which he presented to one of his churchwardens, James Daglass, on leaving Walsingham in 1888[6] – and by the fact that he later edited a book of poetry and prose illustrated by old master pictures. Otherwise his interests in this direction seem to have been largely confined to the setting out and ornamentation of the printed page.

The surviving service registers at Chelmondiston only commence in 1895, the year after Woodward left, and so there is no evidence as to the liturgical changes which he may have made there. Most probably the pattern of services would have been much the same as that which he had inaugerated at Walsingham, with a frequent celebration of the Eucharist, and with services which were fully choral. The latter is certainly suggested by the Terrier made in his final year at Chelmondiston, which lists amongst the possessions of the church twenty-two sets of cassocks and surplices, eight for men and fourteen for boys. But it is unlikely that either the worship or the furnishings were especially elaborate: the same terrier lists just two Altar candlesticks (rather than the six which would be starting to appear in the more ritualistically 'advanced' churches of the period) and, more surprisingly, just three Altar frontals are listed, two white and one red, rather than a complete set of the four principal liturgical colours which might have been expected by this time.[7]

It would seem that Woodward's musical interests at Chelmondiston, as at Walsingham, were not confined to the church building. It was reported for instance in *The Suffolk Chronicle* for January 27th 1894 that 'a large audience assembled in the National Schoolroom on Wednesday evening to listen to a Concert given by members of the Choral Class and their friends. The glees by the class were conducted by the Revd G. R. Woodward.' It would be interesting to know whether he inaugurated this village choral class, and whether he regularly conducted it; if so, it would suggest the continuing influence of John Farmer at Harrow, and the 'house singing' of glees and songs which Woodward had apparently enjoyed as a schoolboy.

Woodward's marriage to Alice Dorothy Lee Warner took place shortly after his institution to Chelmondiston. The wedding was not held at Walsingham, but at St Barnabas' Pimlico, a place which would continue to play a significant part in Woodward's life until the end of the century. A newspaper account of the wedding related that this was where he had 'for eight years laboured most zealously as senior curate', and where, at the wedding service, 'the presence of a numerous congregation – including former Sunday School Scholars – testified to the appreciative feeling of the good work carried out by Mr Woodward during his ministerial career in a populous metropolitan district'. The marriage service was conducted by the Vicar of St Barnabas', the Revd Alfred Gurney; it was 'fully choral' and appropriately the psalm was sung to plainsong. His friend G. H. Palmer was the organist; he played selections from 'Lohengrin' before the service and the Mendelssohn 'Wedding March' afterwards. The newspaper report further relates that:

> The charming bride, who was escorted and given away by her brother, Mr C. B. Lee Warner, was attired in a dress of white corded silk, trimmed with Mechlin lace, her richly-brocaded train being borne by Master Claude Eaton, nephew of Mr Woodward, the handsome little page wearing a Venetian-like costume of crimson plush, with white vest and point-lace collar. Miss Lee Warner's veil was of tulle, her wreath of real orange blossom, her ornaments of pearl, and her magnificent bouquet was chiefly composed of eucharis lilies and lilies of the valley.

There were six bridesmaids, including two of Dorothy's sisters, and all of them were given a gold cross engraved with monogram and date by the bridegroom. The report concludes:

> Mrs Septimus Lee Warner, the bride's mother, provided a *Recherche* champagne breakfast at her temporary London residence, 146 Buckingham Palace Road, where she, later in the day, held a reception. The bridecake, a masterpiece of the confectionery art, was supplied by Buszard, Oxford Street, and was ornamented with real orange blossom and arum lilies. Mr and Mrs Woodward were driven away shortly after two o'clock for Paddington Station, *en route* for Dartmouth, where the honeymoon is to be spent. Rice was showered upon them – as it was when they left the church – accompanied by every good wish that the heart could pray for. Mrs Woodward's travelling gown was of seal-brown cloth, trimmed with beaver fur, and jacket and hat to match. The presents numbered about 360, and were exceedingly chaste and valuable.

A large number of Lee Warner relations, connections, and neighbours attended, as did 'Mr Bayes' – presumably the Walsingham bee-keeper. There appear to have been considerably fewer of Woodward's own family present. His best man was Hopton Stewart, son of his half-sister Annie by her first marriage; she was now married to the Revd W. F. Eaton, who assisted at the service, and it was their son Claude who was pageboy. But there is no mention in the newspaper account of Woodward's brother and sister, Basil and Nellie, having been present. His father had died two years earlier, and if his step-mother was still alive she was most probably prevented from attending by ill-health. The fact that the honeymoon was spent at Dartmouth may perhaps suggest that she was still at 'Glenorleigh', and was visited there. Many years later Woodward would urge a newly-married couple in a wedding sermon to 'study and peruse that delightful, romantic history of young Tobit & Sarah his wedded, as written in the Apocrypha in the Book of Tobit' during their honeymoon. Whether he and Alice 'studied and perused' the book during their stay at Dartmouth is not recorded.

Not long after their return to Chelmondiston, Woodward and his wife travelled to Kent to be present at another wedding. Described in the *Sevenoaks Telegraph* under the heading 'Grand Wedding at Sevenoaks', this was the marriage of Violet Stewart, daughter of Annie, Woodward's half-sister by her first marriage, with Henry Leeke Horsfall, son of Thomas Berry Horsfall M.P. of Bellamour, Rugeley, Staffordshire. Many years earlier, in December 1858, Woodward had been taken to lunch at Bellamour – which was situated near to James Tyrer's home at Tixall – on his tenth birthday, a birthday which he shared with Henry's sister Jessie, and this marriage between his step-niece and a member of a family he had known for so long must have been a particularly happy occasion for him. The bride's brother Hopton Stewart, having been best man at Woodward's wedding, gave the bride away on this occasion, whilst Woodward assisted the Revd W. F. Eaton, Annie's second husband, in the conducting of the wedding service. The present list records that Woodward gave the bride a pearl and amethyst pendant. Despite the grandeur of the occasion – the Marchioness of Abergavenny was amongst the guests – it was not without mishap insofar as the marquee which had been erected on the lawn for the wedding breakfast blew over due to the 'heavy winds'. This, however, did not prevent the performance of a string band which had been brought down from London, whilst it was also recorded, somewhat curiously, that 'the inspiring strains of a bagpipe also enlivened the proceedings considerably'.[8]

As we have seen, Woodward's interest in carols dates back
to at least his early years in Walsingham. But it was during
his years at Chelmondiston that he first began to publish
collections of carols, in which the tunes, harmonised in these
early collections by his friends, were accompanied by words
which he had either translated from the Latin or German or
else composed himself. Traditional carols, which reached
their full development as popular religious songs in the
fifteenth-century and which in their origin were intrinsically
associated with dancing,[9] never seem to have entirely died
out in England. Their general use, however, declined from
the mid-seventeenth century onwards, and by the early
decades of the nineteenth-century some writers considered
that their decline had become terminal. There were various
attempts to preserve and augment them, not all of these
happy, of which perhaps the most influential was the book
*Christmas Carols Old and New* compiled by The Revd H. R.
Bramley and Dr John Stainer, both of Magdalen College,
Oxford, and published in 1871. Some years earlier though,
in 1853, a small book edited by The Revd Thomas Helmore
and The Revd J. M. Neale had appeared. It was entitled
*Carols for Christmas-Tide*, and it contained just twelve
carols. In a 'Notice' at the beginning of the book the editors
wrote 'It is here sufficient to observe: that the original words
and music range from the end of the twelfth-century to the
beginning of the fifteenth-century: that we give the music
without alteration: and that the words are free imitations, for
the most part, of these and other ancient Christmas carols'.
Here was an approach which was rather different from other
attempts to revive the carol; it was scholarly, and it had a
decidely antiquarian feel about it: 'imitations' of 'ancient
Christmas carols' – here we are unmistakably in the world of
the Gothic revival. Woodward's veneration of J. M. Neale
has already been referred to, and the carol book which
his 'master' had produced in 1853 was clearly the inspiration for his own first publication. It has precisely the
same title – *Carols for Christmas-tide* (including the
hyphen) – and it too contained just twelve carols. It is hardly
likely that these similarities occurred by chance; rather
Woodward seems to have been deliberately imitating Neale,

or perhaps more correctly, seeking to continue his 'master's' work, which had been curtailed by Neale's death at the age of forty-eight.

Woodward's *Carols for Christmas-tide*, published in 1892, has an ancient wood-cut of the Virgin and Child reproduced on its cover, in the corner of which the title of the book has been ingeniously incorporated, and the 'mediaevel' feel which this wood-cut introduces is not diminished by his use of the archaic 'long S' (which looks like a small-case 'F', the letter in fact which printers sometimes used to reproduce it) nor indeed by the words of the carols. These verses fall into three groups. For the first two carols the mediaeval Latin words are given, although the second of the two, '*Puer Natus in Bethlehem*', is followed by a translation. This leads to the second type, which is made up of ancient carols translated by Woodward, and it includes his translation of '*Puer Nobis Nascitur*', beginning:

> Unto us is born a Son,
>     King of Quires supernal,
> See on earth his life begun,
>     Of lords the Lord eternal.[10]

Many continue to prefer this to the later translation made by Percy Dearmer beginning 'Unto us a boy is born', and it is Woodward's translation which appears for example in the widely-used modern book *The Celebration Hymnal*. The third type is made up of words newly composed by Woodward. One such is:

> Noel, Noel! Good news I tell,
> And eke a wonder-story:
> A Virgin mild hath borne a Child,
> Jesus, the King of Glory.
>
> Ave Marie ! O well is thee,
> Thou daughter dear of Anna:
> Before thy Son, that holy One,
> Archangels sing Osanna.
>
> Then bells be rung, and mass be sung,
> To greet this kingly Stranger:
> Th'Ancient of days, mankind to raise,
> Abhorreth not the manger.[11]

This is fairly typical of the style in which Woodward would continue to write, a style which has both strengths and weaknesses. The archaisms and a certain forcing of the rhyme – neither of these things irritatingly prevalent in this particular carol – are amongst its weaknesses, whilst the terseness of expression and the strong rhythms, typical of the genuine mediaeval carols which Woodward studied and more usually translated into English – these can be counted as strengths. As, too, must be the fact that the carols which he wrote were for the most part unquestionably carols, rather than the kind of Christmas hymns which some others wrote and which have been incorrectly categorised as carols. To which, finally, must be added the fact that like the medi- aeval Christmas carol, his original productions concentrate on simple expressions – and expressions which are often striking and homely – of the fact of the Incarnation of the divine Word. Sir Richard Terry, in the preface to his *Two Hundred Folk Carols* published in 1922, stressed that the genuine Christmas carol should concern itself with this rather than with 'holly and ivy, robins and snowflakes, roast beef and beer'. Terry must certainly have approved of Woodward's Christmas carols on this particular score.[12] Yet ultimately, perhaps, the critic would say that whilst Woodward did perhaps write a pseudo-mediaeval carol rather well, the value of any kind of pastiche must always remain open to question.

An important consequence of this first collection of carols was Woodward's meeting with Charles Wood, and the estab- lishment of a friendship, and in time of a partnership, which would continue until Wood's death in 1926. In a letter written to Wood in 1923, Woodward recalled 'Again, I am more than ever grateful for your assistance and skill in harmonising my work; ever since the day when as an under- graduate (in Gonville Court) you kindly pointed out some errors in my first venture, and said that, if I ever printed any more, you would run through the proof sheet and see that they were correct'.[13] At this time Charles Wood, who had been born in Ireland in 1866 and had come to England in 1883 to study at the Royal College of Music, was Organ Scholar at Gonville and Caius; in 1894 he became a fellow of

the College – the first music fellow of any Cambridge college
– and also University Lecturer in Harmony and Counter-
point. This meeting of Woodward and Wood came to benefit
both men; for Woodward it was the acquisition of a
conducive and most competent and kindly hand to guide his
musical ventures, whilst for Wood the enthusiasm for plainsong which Woodward conveyed to him would come to have
a particular influence on his later compositions.[14]

A year later, in 1893, Woodward published a further
collection of carols, *Carols for Christmas-tide, Series II.* In
this second book there were just nine items, of which he
wrote by way of introduction 'Where not otherwise stated,
the words of these carols are either written or translated by
the Revd G. R. Woodward' – rather a curious thing to say in
view of the fact that all of them were in fact written or translated by him! More precisely there is just one original composition, 'Come Listen to My Story. This is a charming piece,
relatively free from those features which sometimes marred
his verse, and yet unmistakably in his characteristic pseudo-
mediaeval style. The final two verses read:

> Then rode iii kings together
>   Over desert, hill, and dale;
> Nought caring for the weather,
>   Sleet, and snow, and hail.
> They came from far, led by a star,
>   With beams that never vary;
> *Eya!* full fain they are
>   To see the Babe of Mary.
>
> Away then banish sorrow;
>   *Nato regi psallite:*
> Sith Christ is born this morrow,
>   *Benedicite.*
> With Angels eke and shepherds meek,
>   And with yon Eastern Sages,
> *Eya!* let us go seek
>   The new-born King of ages.[15]

Often, as here, Woodward followed the late-mediaeval
custom of interposing Latin words and phrases into his carol
compositions, such words and phrases usually being taken
from popular Office Hymns. For the mostpart he did this

reasonably sparing, but there is rather more Latin than usual in his translation of '*In Dulci Jubilo*', which appeared in this second collection and which has not tended to find favour with later compilers, due in part, perhaps, to the less than felicitous verse which reads:

> O *Jesus parvule,*
> I yearn for thee always:
> Listen to my ditty,
> O *puer optime,*
> Have pity on me, pity:
> O *princeps glorie,*
> *Trahe me post te.*[16]

Concerning the music for this 1893 collection, Woodward wrote at the beginning of the book 'Mr Chas. Wood, Mr B. Luard Selby, the Revd G. H. Palmer, and especially the Revd J. R. Lunn are hereby thanked by the Editor for their help with the music'. Lunn's being thanked 'especially' is understandable since the book contained five of his harmonisations; there are four from J. S. Bach, two by Luard Selby, and one by Woodward's friend Palmer. Interestingly in view of the extent to which they would work together in the future, there is just one harmonisation by Charles Wood, and equally worthy of note in view of the number or harmonisations he would provide for his future collections, there are none by Woodward himself.

In 1854, the year after Helmore and Neale published their *Carols for Christmas-tide*, they produced a further volume called *Carols for Easter-tide*, which in the nineteenth-century was something of a pioneer in its recognition that not all carols relate to the one festival of Christmas. Given Woodward's veneration for Neale, it is not surprising that his own next production, in 1894, was a volume entitled *Carols for Easter and Ascension-tide*. Once again there were twelve items; again there were two translations from the German (Woodward, following Neale, did not confine himself to old Latin words) and again there was just one new composition. He justified this last by noting that it had 'Words written expressly for the melody of an old Dutch Easter Carol'. Justification was unnecessary, for it was one of his happiest compositions, 'This Joyful Eastertide'. After 'Ding Dong!

Merrily on High' it is almost certainly the most widely known and used of his carols, appearing in a number of contemporary hymnals including *The New English Hymnal*, which also contains one of the translations from the 1894 book, his 'Hail, Easter bright in glory dight!' The same group of musicians again assisted Woodward by providing harmonisations, with the addition of W. H. Frere, although this time there was only one harmonisation by Lunn. Bertram Luard Selby (1853–1918), who had been Organist at St Barnabas' Pimlico since 1887, and who remained there until he became Organist of Rochester Cathedral in 1900, took the lead with five harmonisations; Wood still had only two, and although there were just two harmonisations by Bach, Woodward nevertheless noted as editor that 'For the harmonies he is indebted, first and foremost, to the skill and labours of Joh. Seb. Bach ...' Again Palmer contributed just one harmonisation. Quite how Woodward worked as regards the gathering of these harmonisations – whether he first chose the carols to be included in the collection, and then invited a particular person to harmonise a particular carol – is unfortunately no longer known.

Alongside the work connected with these first small collections of carols, Woodward was also pursuing his interest in plainsong, and of special interest is the chance survival of a letter written by him to an unknown clergyman on March 21st 1894.[17] It is headed Chelmondiston, and he writes:

> Dear Brother,
>     Always very pleased if I can be of any help to you or anybody else *in plano cantu*. I send you the Sarum form of *Tantum ergo & O Salutaris*. The Sarum Hymn Melodies were set up in type by my friend Rev. Theo Mayo, & were given to the London Greg. Choral Ass. They are now out of print, & I myself am aspiring to the honour of reprinting them afresh on better type. I have begun at the Index – cart before the horse you will say.
>     If you want to see Specimens of the type that I wish & hope to use, and the kind of work that is being done in the way of Plainsong, write to
>                         Sister Emma,
>                         S.Mary's, Wantage –

She will enclose you samples of their exquisite printing. They are busy printing the Psalter pointed once & for all, so that any tone & any ending may be sung to any Psalm or Canticle. Also they are hard at work at Tone tables, re-printing Masses, Sequences, Antiphons to Magnificat, Ambrosian tones and what not. All under Palmer & Frere's guidance, & their work does them the utmost credit.

Sister Emma will send you a sample, especially if you mention my name, & send her a 1/- or so, for their expenses are great.

You ask are these Hymns in H.A.&M. The words, of course are to be found in 205, 309, and 311 – But they happen to have hit on the Mechlin forms of these old melodies, & Mechlin is notoriously the most corrupt modern use.

You should join the Plain Song & Mediaeval Society, & then you would see what is being done in Gregorian Music.

The singing in the Sisters' Chapel at Wantage is lovely, so I am told.

If you want to see a good Antiphoner or Gradual, & to read the best Benedictine works on Plainsong, I should think you could not do better than order some of the Solesmes editions, by Dom Pothier.

I heartily wish you also every blessing, you and your people, both now & at Easter.

Yours very truly in Xp,
G. R. Woodward

Woodward's enthusiasm for plainsong is seen very clearly in this letter, as too is the fact that he was actively involved at this time in its revival and promotion. The book of Sarum Hymn Melodies which he mentions does not seem to have been completed and published. W. H. Frere edited *Plainsong Hymn-melodies*, which was published by the Plainsong and Mediaeval Music Society in 1896, and the knowledge that Frere was working in this field may well have stopped the self-effacing Woodward from continuing with his own edition. It is interesting that he is very much aware of the pioneering work being carried out at Wantage; doubtless he was kept informed by G. H. Palmer, who played an important part in that work. Interesting too that by now he was very critical of the Mechlin use, having used a plainsong psalter which favoured it during his first years at Walsingham a decade earlier. Probably this was due, as the

letter suggests, to his coming into contact with the work of
Solesmes and Dom Pothier, possibly through W. J. Birkbeck.
Perhaps a clearer example of Woodward's self-effacement
would be the fact that no mention is made of a scholarly
work which he published jointly with G. H. Palmer in the
year in which the letter was written: *The Canticles at Mattins
and Evensong Pointed to the Eight Gregorian Tones as given
in the Sarum Tonale.* This would seem to have been
published as a companion to Palmer's *The Psalms of David
Pointed to the Eight Gregorian Tones as given in the Sarum
Tonale,* which had finally been published in that same year,
Palmer describing himself on the title-page as 'Sometimes
Master of the Quire at St Barnabas', Pimlico'. Like his friend,
Palmer always seems to have used 'Quire' rather than
'Choir', and to have retained the use of the archaic 'long S'.

The letter quoted above is written on black-edged
notepaper, the reason for this being that Alice Dorothy
Woodward had died a few months earlier, on September 21st
1893. According to the brief notice which appeared in the
*Lynn Advertiser* her death had taken place at Pangbourne.
She was just thirty-three, and there had been no children by
the marriage. In death as in life she remains a shadowy
figure, almost all that is known of her now coming from the
newspaper account of her wedding. Her body was brought
back to Walsingham for burial, and over her grave
Woodward erected a granite celtic cross with the inscription:

Here lyeth
ALICE DOROTHY WOODWARD
who fell asleep on the Feast of
St Matthew AD 1893
AGED 33
*Fili Dei, Misere Mei*

The use of the word 'lyeth', the 'long S' in misere, the Latin
prayer, and the dating by a feast of the Church[18] are all
typical Woodward mannerisms.

In the following year, it was reported in *The Suffolk
Chronicle* for November 10th that 'At the close of his
sermon on Sunday the Rector, the Revd G. R. Woodward,
announced that he had resigned the living and had accepted
the offer of Assistant Priest and Precentor at the Church of St

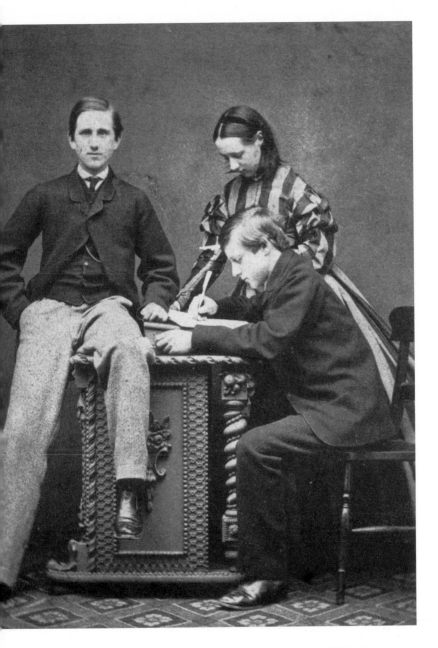

G. R. Woodward (left) in the late eighteen-sixties, with his sister
Helen (Nellie) and his brother Basil.

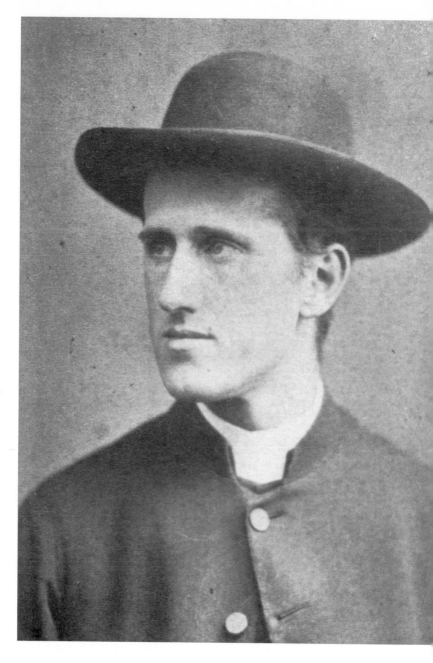

G. R. Woodward as a young priest at St Barnabas' Pimlico in the
late eighteen-seventies.

Barnabas', Pimlico'. Woodward was forty-six years old when he left Chelmondiston, and he would hold no further incumbency. It is possible that his wife's death had affected him in such a way that he felt no inclination to continue working in a parish on his own – although more than a year had in fact elapsed between her death and his resignation. Again it may have been that he now felt free to pursue his particular literary and musical interests without the need to augment his private financial resources by an incumbent's stipend. St Barnabas' had always, one suspects, exercised a considerable pull on his loyalty and affections, and in many ways it offered an ideal base for his researches. The days when he had played a full and lively part in parish and village life were now largely over, and whilst he was far from becoming a recluse after 1894 – especially during the next few years when he held a series of three curacies – he would nevertheless spend much of the remainder of his life moving in a fairly small circle of like-minded people, pursuing his studies, his verse compositions and translations, seeing to his publications, and fulfilling his spiritual obligations as a priest in the Church of England, but taking little part in public life or society. His *Carols for Easter and Ascension-tide* were dedicated 'In Memoriam A.D.W.', and possibly he was thinking about her when he wrote the final section of the long narrative poem 'Legend of St Dorothy' which concluded his *Legends of the Saints*, published five years after her death. He wrote there of St Dorothy, his wife's namesake – somewhat wistfully, perhaps –

> May we too join her company
> And make good ending when we die:
> Be ours to win that heavenly home,
> The fields of Paradise to roam,
> Where noble fruits and flowers abound,
> And true and endless joys are found,
> Where seemly angels sit and sing
> And merrily the bells do ring,
> Where day and night the heavenly host
> Bless Father, Son, and Holy Ghost. *Amen.*[19]

# CHAPTER FIVE

# LONDON 1894–1901

Throughout the twelve years which Woodward spent in East Anglia, first as Vicar of Walsingham and then as Rector of Chelmondiston, he seems to have kept up his links with St Barnabas' Pimlico, and so when he returned to London in 1894, chiefly, it seems, to be better able to pursue his literary and musical interests, it was not wholly surprising that he should have returned to this particular parish. It was familiar to him, and he seems to have been held in affection there; also its musical and liturgical tradition expressed and fulfilled his own ideals. Alfred Gurney, who had officiated at Woodward's marriage five years earlier, was still the incumbent in 1894, and would remain there until 1898.

Gurney was a prolific writer of poetry and prose; in 1896 the printer and booksellers Messrs H. Grice, who had an establishment in the parish, were listing no less than six of his books in their advertisement in the parish magazine. These had the varied titles of *Daydreams: The Story of a Friendship; The Vision of the Eucharist; A Christmas Faggot; Our Catholic Inheritance in the Larger Hope; Wagner's Parsifal;* and *Voices from The Holy Sepulchre and Other Poems.* It is interesting to note Gurney's apparent interest in Wagner, which he may have passed on to Woodward when they worked together at St Barnabas' between 1879 and 1882, and which Woodward afterwards shared with Mrs Septimus Lee Warner and her daughters at 'Lohengrin Lodge'. It may to have been Gurney who encouraged him to write poetry, since his first book of poems, *Legends of the Saints*, was published during the last year in which they worked together.

Gurney was one of those wealthy Anglo-catholic incumbents who used his private resources to provide fine furnishings for his church, and when Woodward returned to St Barnabas' in 1894 it was to a building with a considerably enriched interior. In those intervening years it had, according to one writer, been 'gradually refitted in truly sumptuous

style'[1] under the direction of that most sensitive of late nineteenth-century architects G. F. Bodley, who had, as we have
seen, recently been working at Chelmondiston. Bodley was
not infrequently employed to realise the dreams of wealthy
Anglo-catholic patrons, most memorably perhaps by the 7th
Duke of Newcastle at Clumber Chapel in 1886–1889 and,
somewhat earlier, by Mrs Meynell-Ingram at Hoar Cross in
1871–1876. At Pimlico his first work was the crypt chapel
in 1887, which was followed by the High Altar reredos in
1893, and later by the organ case and the particularly
beautiful chancel screen. As at Clumber Chapel, certain
furnishings were added by John Ninian Comper (1864–
1960), who, like Woodward, had been married at St
Barnabas'; these included the fine sacrament house,
designed, apparently, in the 1890s,[2] even though perpetual
reservation of the Blessed Sacrament did not begin until
1901, after both Gurney and Woodward had left.

But if the decor of the church to which Woodward
returned had changed, the pattern and character of the
worship was little altered from how it had been during his
first period as a curate there, apart from the introduction of
the use of incense in 1894. On weekdays there was a
Eucharist at 7.00 am. (it is significant that although St
Barnabas' was considered an 'advanced' church, the name
'Mass' does not appear in the parish magazine during this
period, nor does the address 'Father'), followed by Mattins
at 8.00 am, and with Evensong at 6.00 pm. On Sundays,
Eucharists were celebrated at 7.00 am and 8.00 am, with
Mattins and Sermon at 10.30 am followed by the 'Solemn
Celebration' at 11.45 am. Later in the day there was a
Children's Service at 3.30 pm and Evensong and Sermon at
7.00 pm. Naturally the worship was centred upon the
Eucharist, and eucharistic worship and devotion was encouraged by a Ward of the Confraternity of the Blessed
Sacrament and by the monthly Preparation Service for Holy
Communion which took place on the Monday before each
first Sunday of the month. There were Stations of the Cross
each first Friday, and separate Bible Classes each week for
lads, men, women, and Sunday School teachers. Rather
surprisingly and disappointingly, very little is said in the

parish magazines about the music used at the services, and one of the very few references to music concerns not the liturgical choir, but the St Barnabas Choral Society. Following its formation at the end of 1896, this society rehearsed every Monday evening, and again as at Chelmondiston, one suspects that Woodward may have played a significant part in the formation and activities of the group.

The general impression of St Barnabas' during these years 1894–1899 is of an active and efficiently-run parish. Gurney was assisted by four curates, who lived at various addresses rather than in the original clergy house built by Bennett. Woodward lived at 24 Alderney Street, a fairly modest three-storey terraced house in one of the long streets which run parallel to each other between Warwick Way and Lupus Street. Each curate had his own 'district' within the parish: Woodward's, which included parts of Pimlico Road, Eaton Terrace, and Graham Street seems to have been in the more affluent part of it, perhaps in deference to his age and seniority – he was forty-six when he returned to London.

Again each curate was assisted by a team of District Visitors, Woodward's being made up of five women including Lady Maria Howard, in addition to Sisters from the Mission House. In another of the teams was a Miss Skinner, and since her address is that of Mr Charles Skinner and his wife Lady Kathleen, 57 Eccleston Square, it seems likely that Miss Skinner was a daughter of Frances Mary Skinner and a sister of Charles. In view of the book dedications to the Skinners already mentioned, and the fact that both Charles and his sister seem to have been active in the parish – Charles for example addressing the parish branch of the Church of England Working Men's Society at their anniversary in 1896 – it would seem likely that Woodward was on close terms with the family, and indeed they may have suggested his return to Pimlico in the same way that they may have played a part in his earlier excursion into Suffolk. It appears from the contemporary parish magazines that Woodward played a fairly full part in parish life. He would have visited in his specific area, he ran a Bible class for women on Wednesday afternoons, 3.00 pm to 4.00 pm in the St Barnabas Institute – requesting in the magazine that those attending should bring pencil and notebook – and on Christmas Day 1895 he conducted four out of the five weddings which took place at St Barnabas'.

Meanwhile his work with carols continued, and in 1897, three years after *Carols and Hymns for Easter and Ascension-tide*, he published *Hymns and Carols for Christmas-tide*, which was 'dutifully and affectionately' dedicated to Alfred Gurney. It contained twenty-eight items, some of which as he said in the Preface, had already appeared in his two earlier Christmas collections. If this collection is seen as the forerunner of his most successful work *The Cowley Carol Book*, then some of the points which he makes in the Preface to the 1897 book are particularly interesting. Having praised the pioneering work of Neale and Helmore, and having explained that his need to translate and write words for certain tunes was due to the unwillingness of contemporary poets to write verses in unusual metres – a theme to which he would return in the Preface to the 'Second Series' of *The Cowley Carol Book* in 1919 – he then goes on to write more fully and freely than he would do anywhere else about his own feelings regarding ancient carols. He says:

> These carols in their original language at any rate, will be found to have an indescribable charm, being so simple and *naive*, and yet so profound. They have a genuine Catholick 'ring' about them, and they breathe of the old world. The Editor is aware that they will not appeal to all: but if they find their way into the hearts of some, and help in any way to emphasise the doctrine of the Incarnation of our Lord Jesus Christ and the worship due to him, if they tend to the honour of His mother Mary, and if they prove an aid to those who love to celebrate the Birthday of the Holy Child, then the Editor's labour will be amply rewarded.[3]

Here, as in few other places, Woodward – who maintained that characteristic Tractarian 'reserve' in speaking openly about spiritual matters – significantly admits to having the intention of encouraging devotion to Jesus and Mary through his work. He also betrays here that romantic approach to ancient things which recurs later in the Preface: 'The writers of these Carols were the contemporaries of the men who built Durham Cathedral and Westminster Abbey, who painted the windows in York Minster, and illuminated the manuscripts which we still see and admire in the British Museum'.

The words in *Hymns and Carols for Christmas-tide* are almost all translations from the Latin and German (translations from the Greek came only in later collections) with the single exception of his own composition *Come Listen to My Story*, which had first appeared in the 1893 collection. But published here for the first time was his translation of *Quem Pastores*, which perhaps due to the popularity of the words which Percy Dearmer later wrote to accompany the tune, has not passed into general use. Woodward's translation reads:

> Whom of old the shepherds praisèd,
> When the Seraph them upraisèd,
> Saying, 'Sirs, be not amazèd;
>   Natus est Rex gloriae':
>
> Unto whom the Kings came faring
> Gold in hand, myrrh, incense, bearing,
> Love unfeignedly declaring
>   Leoni victoriae:
>
> Him with Mary bless, nor tire
> Chanting with the angelic quire:
> High uplift the strain, and higher,
>   Laus, honor et gloriae.
>
> To the Christ-child, King of heaven,
> God, to man through Mary given,
> Raise the lay from morn till even,
>   Dulci cum melodia.[4]

Engagingly, he places the following verse at the end of the book, claiming it, not wholly convincingly, to be anonymous:

> Pray for him, both old and young,
> That turned this book to English tongue;
> Whoso he be and in what stead,
> Whether he live or he be dead.[5]

In the British Library there are four sheets, now bound together but originally sold separately at one penny each, headed *Easter Carols*. Undated, the library catalogue suggests that they were published in 1900, but they may date from sometime during the period 1894–1899 when Woodward was at St Barnabas', having been printed by the firm of H. Grice which was based in Pimlico and which published his *Hymns and Carols for Christmas-tide* in 1897. There may of course have been more than just the four single sheets which survive. Of these, the words are all translations, two from the Latin and two from German, and none of them had appeared in the 1894 book *Carols for Easter and Ascension-tide*. The harmonisation of one carol is by Luard Selby, the other three being by Woodward himself. These items are significant because it is here, apparently, that Woodward first makes his appearance as a composer, and not simply a collector, of harmonisations.[6]

It was in this period of his life that Woodward wrote the first three of the various collections of verse which he would continue to produce from time to time, and although the second and third were published just outside the years covered by this chapter, in 1902 and 1903, it may be best to consider the three collections together. Mention has already been made to the one published in 1898 and dedicated to Frances Mary Skinner, which was called *Legends of The Saints*. It is in three parts, Part III being the seventeen-page-long 'Legend of St Dorothy'. Part I contains eleven legends, varying in length. The first, 'The Legend of St Christopher', is an original composition of nineteen pages; some others appear to be translations, but the sources of these are not indicated. Amongst the latter is 'St Ursula', which has the somewhat stilted refrain

> Maid Ursula, now as of yore
> Be likewise thou our commodore,
> And land us on the heavenly shore.

Part II is headed 'Other verses' and contains seventeen short items. Rather surprisingly in view of the title of the volume these verses are on a variety of subjects, and include two hymn-translations, one of them a translation of Nikolai's 'Wachet Auf'. These look forward to the many translations of hymns which would appear in his hymnal *Songs of Syon* six years later. Next, in 1902, came the privately printed *The*

*Seven Sleepers of Ephesus*, dedicated to Lady Kathleen Skinner and her eighteen-year old son Edgar Louis. Perhaps Edgar was rather a favourite of Woodward's, since he is the only one of Lady Kathleen's five children to be included in the dedication. *The Seven Sleepers* is a small book, bound in paper and of just twenty-three pages. The poem is in rhyming couplets, and begins:

> Come, men and maidens, old and young,
> And ye shall hear in English tongue,
> And drawn in simple verse and rime,
> A wonder-tale of olden time,
> When Decius, of bad renown,
> Yet wore the Imperator's crown.
> Sworn enemy, in word and deed,
> Of Christ and his Apostles Creed.[7]

It is an undoubtedly devout work, and in parts spirited, but his 'simple verse and rime' has just the suggestion of a pantomine script. The legend of the Seven Sleepers seems to have fascinated him, the Preface to the revised and enlarged edition of his important work *Songs of Syon* being dated 'Feast of the vii Sleepers of Ephesus'. Could he possibly have felt that he, like the seven men in the legend, really belonged to another age and had woken up in a world which seemed strangely alien? There were certainly those to whom he would give that impression later in life.[8]

The third and most substantial of the three books of verse, *Poemata*, was published in 1903; it was hard-bound, and extended to one hundred and seventy-eight pages. The first section, 'From the Greek' contains forty-three items; the next, 'From the Latin', eleven times; 'From the German' has forty-four items; 'From the French' just three items; and 'Original', eight items. Most of the book is therefore made up of translations from foreign verse into English, whilst the comparative sizes of the sections draws attention to the fact that here and elsewhere Woodward showed hardly any interest in making translations from the French, nor, indeed, in any aspect of French culture. Apart from this limitation, the wide field from which he chose his subjects for transla-tion indicates the considerable breadth both of his reading and appreciation, whilst one poem in the 'Original' section

gives a further insight into his very conservative and sometimes pessimistic outlook. It is called 'All the Foundations of
the Earth are Out of Course', and having begun ...

> The world heigho! from foot to crown
> Is topsy-turvey, up-so-down.

it finally concludes

> The times are sadly out of joint.
> Now plainly hear my story's point.
> Wo worth the day, dear Angle-land,
> When lower things gain upper hand:
> When youth is held more wise than age,
> And *ignoramus* schooleth sage:
> When mob-law reigns, and might is right;
> Sweet callèd bitter, darkness light.
> Absurd and wrong it were, nay worse,
> The laws of nature to reverse,
> When hands and arms and feet below
> Inform the head which way to go;
> When rabblement dare legislate
> For prince and peasant, Church and State.
> When man will live and die like beast.
> When lay-folk think to teach the priest;
> When small and great, in hearth and hall,
> Make self and Mammon all in all:-
> Then head to foot, and toe to crown
> The world is turnèd up-so-down.[9]

But if this poem illustrates one aspect of Woodward's
outlook and indeed personality, then another is shown in his
translation from a Latin verse written by J. A. Holthevfer in
1551, which ends:

> Musick can soothe the trouble breast,
> And lull the care-worn frame to rest:
> 'Tis heard alike in banquet hall,
> And sacred buildings, great and small.
>
> Musick, afloat on heavenly wing
> To God and man doth solace bring:
> Dear are the folk that musick love
> To man below and God above.[10]

Woodward's second period at St Barnabas' ended in 1899.
Alfred Gurey had left in the previous year, and had been

succeeded by the Revd the Hon. A. F. A. Hanbury Tracy, who would remain in Pimlico until 1927. There seems no reason to suppose that it was the change in incumbency which cause Woodward to leave; Hanbury Tracy would write about him graciously, admiring, even affectionately in the parish magazine both in 1919 when his *Saint George Megalomartyr* was published and again in 1924 when he received the Lambeth doctorate of Music, giving no suggestion that there had even been ill-feeling between them. The reason for his departure was probably that he wanted to devote himself wholly to the preparation of what would be his best-known (and in those terms, most successful) work, *The Cowley Carol Book*, which made its first appearance in 1901. This became, and remained for many years, the most popular English carol book until it was somewhat eclipsed by the *Oxford Carol Book*, published in 1928, and then finally superseded in common use by the series of *Carols for Choirs* which began in 1961. As with his first publication, *Carols for Christmastide*, there was a First and a Second Series. The first, published in 1901 consisted of thirty-nine carols, several of which were again taken from his earlier collections; this First Series had a second edition in the following year, when the number increased to sixty-five. The appearance of the Second Series, which had been intended for Christmas 1914, was delayed by the First World War, but when it was published in 1919 it added a further thirty-seven carols to the collection. Woodward edited the first series alone; for the second, Charles Wood acted as co-editor. As the number of carols indicates, *The Cowley Carol Book* was a much larger undertaking than the earlier collections. Mowbrays were the publishers, and presumably at their insistence Woodward's preferred use of the 'long S' was here happily abandoned.

Woodward began his Preface to the second edition of *The Cowley Carol Book, First Series*, by stating that the collection had originated in a request that he should 'compile a small volume of Carols for use in the Church of St John the Evangelist at Cowley', and it is interesting to speculate on how this request may have come about. The church in question was that of the Society of St John the Evangelist, usually known as the 'Cowley Fathers', which had been built to G. F.

Bodley's designs between 1896 and 1902, and one possible link is, of course, Bodley himself, who had worked for Woodward at Chelmondiston in 1891. Another link which Woodward had with the Society – although again somewhat tenuous – was through his Assistant Curate at Walsingham, the Revd E. F. Elwin, who became a Cowley Father in 1892. But since Elwin spent the remainder of his life after 1896 in India, it is unlikely that he had any involvement with the musical life of the mother house after that year. A third and perhaps more likely link was through Woodward's connection with G. H. Palmer; Palmer became Director of Music at Cowley, and although this was not until 1917, he was apparently unofficially involved with the music at Cowley many years before this.[11]

The second paragraph of the Preface is of particular interest for the light it sheds on the literary side of the collection. Woodward wrote:

> The contents and treasures of those most admirable collections of *Carols for Christmas-tide*, 1853, and *Carols for Easter-tide*, 1854, by the Revd J. M. Neale and the Revd T. Helmore, have again been freely drawn upon. In the New edition (containing sixty-five carols in all) no fewer than twenty-one can claim Dr Neale for their Author. His words are given unaltered, except in one case … where, owing to the exigences of the music, a short Latin phrase has been substituted for two Alleluyas. Concerning the words of the other Carols, some … are in Latin; others … are of old English origin. For the remainder the Editor is himself responsible. They are, for the most part, translations of Latin or German Carols, ranging from the XIIth to the XVIth century. In half a dozen instances, for some fine old melody's sake, the Editor has written words of his own. Fault has been found with the Latin lines which occur here and there interspersed amongst the English verse; but the Editor ventures to think that the rhythm and association of the original tongue is sufficient excuse for this not having altered the arrangement.

His admiration for Neale's work is evident in the fact that a third of the words in the book are his, but Woodward is characteristically modest about his own original compositions, saying that he has only written them 'for some fine old melody's sake'. Here as elsewhere he gives the impression that his primary interest is always in the tune, rather than in

the words which accompany it, and indeed that he sees the
words as subservient to the tune rather than enjoying a parity
of importance with it. This may surprise in view of the fact
that so far as composition is concerned, his original work lay
in the area of the words rather than with the music. Yet
despite his appearing to give only a secondary importance to
the words, he nevertheless seems to have taken considerable
pains with them, and to have enjoyed composing them.

As in the earlier collections, he thanked those who had
provided harmonisations. Luard Selby had again contributed, joined for the first time by W. Shebbeare and E. W.
Goldsmith; the latter was to serve with Woodward for many
years on the council of the Plainsong and Mediaeval Music
Society. Wood and Palmer were given especial thanks, with
the graceful tribute to Wood that since he had revised and
passed the proof-sheets, the user has a 'guarantee of its
correctness'. But when the sources of the harmonisations in
*The Cowley Carol Book, First Series* are examined, there are
several surprises. The first, in view of Woodward's friendship
with Wood, and of their later collaboration, is that out of the
sixty-five carols in the 1902 enlarged edition, only five are
harmonised by Wood; clearly his principal contribution was
indeed the revision of the proof-sheets. Then it is interesting
that Palmer, who only had the odd harmonisation in the
early collections, has six items in this one, whilst Lunn and
Luard Selby, whose harmonisations had figured largely in the
collections of the early 1890s, here only contribute three and
four items respectively. However the major surprise in
comparing *The Cowley Carol Book, First Series* with its
predecessors is the number of harmonisations made by
Woodward himself: from having provided no harmonisations for the earlier collections, he was here responsible for
over thirty – nearly half of those contained in the book. It
seems as though Woodward had discovered in himself a
particular ability, or at least the confidence to use that ability.
For these harmonisations are excellent, and have continued
to win the approval of church musicians. Sir David
Willcocks, for example, himself a master of the art of
harmonising carol tunes, has remarked 'I have a high opinion
of G. R. Woodward's harmonisations of carol melodies ...

they were easily sung by choirs and were invariably in good taste. GRW had obviously either had training as a musician, or possessed a sure instinct for the 'grammar' of musical composition, for he obeyed all the 'rules' of harmony as accepted at that time ... It is possible that Dr Charles Wood, a musical craftsman of the highest order, may have made suggestions to GRW when correcting proofs, but I have no evidence that GRW needed help or advice over his work, either from the literary or musical standpoint.'[12] Further, as the musicologist Dr Watkins Shaw has pointed out, the very fact that so distinguished a musician as Charles Wood was prepared to collaborate with Woodward on *The Cowley Carol Book*, and with later collections too, is in itself a testimony to Woodward's musical ability.[13] It appears, however, that Woodward's natural modesty caused him to feel some embarrassment over the inclusion of so many of his own harmonisations, since some of them are headed 'Harmony by the Editor of this work' and others 'Harmonized by Revd G. R. Woodward', rather as if two different people were responsible. In view of Woodward's success in this field, it is maybe surprising that when *The Cowley Carol Book, Second Series* appeared in 1919, adding a further thirty-seven carols to the collection, only four of the harmonisations were supplied by him. Charles Wood was co-editor of this Second Series, and he provided well over half of the harmonisations himself; Palmer, Lunn, and Goldsmith each contributed just one.

Whilst J. M. Neale was the writer or translator of one third of the carols in *The Cowley Carol Book, First Series*, and the majority of the remainder were Woodward's translations from the Latin and German, the book did contain, as he wrote in the Preface, some new compositions. One of these which is still heard is 'Up! Good Christen Folk and Listen'; another which is of considerable charm – and which may claim to be one of his more successful pieces – is the cradle-song 'Come, Rock the Cradle for Him':

> Come, rock the cradle for Him,
> Come, in the crib adore Him,
> Dull care, I pray you bury,
> And in the Lord make merry.
> > Sweet little Jesu, sweet little Jesu.

Come, rock his cradle lowly,
The throne of God all-holy:
Come worship and adore Him,
And kneel we down before Him,
   Sweet little Jesu, sweet little Jesu.

Nor come with empty coffer,
But thanks and blessing offer;
Let old and young be merry,
And blithe as bird on berry.
   Sweet little Jesu, sweet little Jesu.

And sing, for music-number
Will lull the Babe to slumber:
Your strain be sweet and airy,
Like that of blessed Mary.
   Sweet little Jesu, sweet little Jesu.

Do nothing to annoy Him,
But everything to joy Him;
For sin, by night or morrow,
Would cause Him pain and sorrow,
   Sweet little Jesu, sweet little Jesu.

So at your hour of dying,
This Babe, in cradle lying,
(For He is King supernal)
Shall grant you rest eternal.
   Sweet little Jesu, sweet little Jesu.[14]

There is nothing here which is mannered, quaint, or senti-
mental, but rather there is an engaging simplicity and
smoothness of rhyme and rhythm which not only suggest the
movement of the cradle, but also show Woodward the versi-
fyer at his best.

As it is interesting to compare the respective sources of the
harmonisations in the two Series of *The Cowley Carol Book*,
so too with the words. Of the thirty-seven additional items in
the second Series, a further six come from J. M. Neale, but
here almost all of the remainder – and hence the large
majority – are Woodward's own work, either as translator or
author. As in the first Series, there are translations from the
Latin and the German, but here there are also several items
translated from the Greek, indicating a new field of interest
which will be examined later. Seven carols have words newly
composed, which represents a higher proportion of the total

than in the first series. Again he offers an explanation – almost an apology – for the number of his own pieces, writing in the 1919 Preface:

> Whenever traditional, original, or translated material happened to be ready at hand (the words exactly agreeing with the metre, rhythm, and character of the music note), then the labour, skill, poetry, and piety of Dr John Mason Neale, and of others, has again been readily laid under contribution. But, because the greater part of the melodies, chosen for this second series of Cowley Carols, demanded words in some peculiar or outlandish measure; and because your modern Carol-writer, as a rule, dislikes being tied down to any unusual or difficult metre, that particular editor of this book, who is chiefly responsible for the selection of the aforesaid tunes, had no alternative but himself to set to work, and translate, or write, fresh carols, such as they are, but anyhow so versified and rimed as to suit the requirements of the music. This is the sole reason for the frequent recurrence of the initials, G. R. W. If there be an old-world ring in some of these new Carol-words, apology is neither needed, nor conceded on the part of the author thereof: for it seems only fitting and appropriate that the words should be in keeping with the somewhat antiquated tunes whereto they have here been wedded.[15]

It is worthwhile quoting this passage at length because it is equally indicative of both Woodward's character and intention. In it we see his diffidence and self-effacement, but alongside this his firmness of conviction, together with his high and exacting standards: the words must agree 'exactly' with the metre, rythm, and character of the music note. And, as ever, we see his veneration for Neale, whose words he clearly considers can never be bettered. But was he, perhaps, not being entirely honest with himself in suggesting that he supplied words for carols almost against his inclination, and certainly only when there was no alternative? Possibly not, for his enjoyment in writing words for carols is seen in the fact that in later life he prepared several small books of such words when there was no apparent need to provide words to accompany a particular tune.

As regards the light which the passage sheds on his particular intention in composing carol-verses, he is again seen giving primacy to the ancient tunes, and maintaining that they must dictate not only the precise form of the words – their metre and rythm – but also their character. It is, he claims, appropriate that tunes dating maybe from the fifteenth or sixteenth centuries should be given words which have an 'old-world' ring, and something which ought to be applauded rather than criticised as being archaic. He is not being eccentric or perverse, he would maintain, in producing the kind of verses which it is so easy to condemn as being 'quaint', but is rather showing artistic sensitivity in seeking to match the one to the other. Hence he would not have agreed unreservedly with the opinion given by Percy Dearmer in the preface to *The Oxford Book of Carols* that 'Carols moreover were always modern ... The charm of an old carol lies precisely in its having been true to the period in which it was written, and those which are alive today retain their vitality because of this sincerity; for imitations are always sickly and short-lived. A genuine carol may have faults of grammar, logic, and prosody; but one fault it never has – that of sham antiquity'.[16]

Perhaps Woodward would have replied that the carol tunes in his collections were, all of them, authentic, and that this is what mattered most; as for the words which he provided when such provision was necessary, these were most certainly 'true to the period' in which the tune had been written, and to have provided some sort of 'contemporary' words would have been to try to put new wine into old skins, which would have been a likely recipe for producing something which was certainly and deservedly 'sickly and short-lived'. He might also have drawn attention to the originality of his 'new' words, and certainly the new compositions are often vigorous, striking, and imaginative rather than simply 'sham-antique'. Thus C. S. Phillips, in comparing Woodward with Neale in his book *Hymnody Past and Present*, notes that both men had a 'curiously mediaeval cast of mind', but that in the translations and compositions in *The Cowley Carol Book* Woodward shows 'a lighter literary touch and a charming quaintness of language and fancy that borders at times on the fantastic'.[17] An example might be a composition which first appeared in the Second Series called 'Of these Four Letters Sing Will I', in which he seems to have made no concession to the earlier criticism of his following the old custom of interspersing the English words with Latin phrases:

> Of these four letters sing will I
>   *In Dulci Melodia*
> Of M and A and R and Y,
>   *De Virgine Maria.*
> For Mother of th' Incarnate Word
>   *Virginitatis Via,*
> Of women none may be preferr'd
>   *Beata Prae Maria.*
>
> Misdoubting not the Father's plan,
>   *Testante Hieremia,*
> 'tis she that compass'd hath a Man,
>   *Conceptum Ope Dia:*
> And, as the Holy Spirit will'd,
>   *Locutus de Messia*
> In her is Esay's word fulfill'd,
>   *Vetusque Prophetia.*
>
> An Angel and of high degree
>   *Celesti in Hierarchia,*
> Came down to greet this Maiden free,
>   *Dicens, 'Ave Maria!*
> Fear not; bedew'd with heav'nly shower
>   *O Virgin, Virgo Pia,*
> Thy bloom shall be th'immortal Flower:
>   *Ne Timeas, Maria.'*
>
> Ride westward kings from Saba, three,
>   *Ferentes Dona Tria,*
> And 'fore the Babe on Mary's knee
>   *Genuflectuntur, Quia*
> 'Twas God, if of his glory shorn,
>   *Cum Genitrice Pia,*
> When God was born on Christmas morn
>   *Ex Virgine Maria.*
>
> Yea therefore, Mary, pray thy Son,
>   *Qui Patris est Sophia,*
> To teach and lead us every one
>   *Ad Ceolica Bravia;*
> Where Quire doth sing and belfrey ring,
>   *Cum Suavi Symphonia,*
> To laud thy Child, O Maiden mild,
>   *Mater Dei, Maria.*[18]

This is a clever as well as an original piece of writing, especially perhaps in the rhymning of both the Latin and English lines, and in the way that the rhymning system of the latter gradually develops in the two final verses. To condemn such a composition as merely sham and insincere would be as unjust as to condemn the best work of the Gothic revival architects in those terms, and would show a similar lack of understanding as regards what the artist was seeking to achieve. This particular carol, written in the second decade of the century, seems to exhibit Woodward's deepening devotion to the Blessed Virgin Mary, a devotion which had probably been fostered by his recent work on the hymns of the Greek Church, and which would continue with him.

The preparation of *The Cowley Carol Book, First Series*, launched in 1901 and followed in 1902 by a second and enlarged edition, must have involved its editor in considerable labour, particularly in view of the very high standards which he set both himself and others. The searching out of old carol tunes in manuscripts and books, the collecting or writing of harmonizations, and the provision of suitable words composed or translated by either himself or others – all this must have required a considerable expenditure of time and energy, and so it is hardly surprising that he felt it necessary to withdraw from full-time parish work in 1899, in just the way that his colleague Palmer had done a decade earlier in order to pursue his own researches in the field of plainsong.

Initially Woodward seems to have continued to live in Alderney Street, which was the address given in the 1901 *List of the Clergy*, although by the following year his address was 7 Shelley Court, Chelsea. Meanwhile, having left St Barnabas' in 1899, he seems to have assisted for the next year or so at the Berkeley Chapel in Mayfair, a large eighteenth-century proprietary chapel, now demolished, which had a tractarian tradition of worship.[19] The incumbent there was the Revd the Hon. James Adderley, younger son of the first Baron Norton. In his book *In Slums and Society*, Adderley speaks of having 'tried my hands for three year at ministry among "the rich"' at the Berkeley Chapel, adding that 'the Services at Berkeley Chapel were very

popular, and I do not think I remember any more fruitful
years of my life than those I spent there. It was quite a new
sensation for me to have grand ladies and gentlemen at my
Bible Class and sermons. It was a motley crowd, and it rather
liked being treated like a congregation of East Enders.'[20] It is
interesting that another priest who was involved with the
Berkeley Chapel at this time was Percy Dearmer, whose well-
known work *The Parson's Handbook* had been published in
1899, and who left the chapel in 1901 to become Vicar of St
Mary's, Primrose Hill, the church with which he is popularly
associated. He and Woodward were very different in
outlook and temperament (not least insofar as Dearmer, like
Adderley, was attracted by Christian Socialism, and, on occasion, inclined towards theological liberalism) and so it is
perhaps not surprising that they should have had a serious
disagreement over a matter of principle a few years later.
This was to be over the compilation of *The English Hymnal*,
but by then Woodward's own remarkable hymnal *Songs of
Syon* would have appeared, and it was to this ambitious
work that he turned after the completion of the first series of
*The Cowley Carol Book*.

# CHAPTER SIX

# LONDON 1901–1916

When James Adderley moved from the Berkeley Chapel to St Mark's Marylebone in 1901, Woodward moved with him, presumably as an honorary assistant curate. They remained there together until 1904, when Adderley moved yet again, this time to take up the family living of Saltley near Birmingham. There seems to be no evidence as to where Woodward worshipped, and maybe assisted, from 1904 until he moved to Highgate in 1916 and began to attend St Augustine's church there. Indeed comparatively little is known of him during these years apart from his considerable musical and literary activities.

Adderley was a well-known, colourful, and unconventional priest, in some ways the complete antithesis to Woodward. He was an extravert, preaching in the open air from costers' barrows and conducting Stations of the Cross on street corners; he travelled extensively to give retreats and conduct missions, and he was a liberal in politics and at times in his theological outlook too. His domestic life was disorganised: Fr Dru Dury, who became his curate at about this time recalled that he lived 'a rough and ready sort of life, which was apt to disconcert members of his household. It didn't appear that he thought cleanliness was next to godliness, and he paid no attention to the quality of the food served at meals ... he was quite uncontrollable.'[1] It is true that he liked church music, and indeed composed hymns, but the kind of church music which he liked apparently 'infuriated' Woodward. But as Fr Drury further recalled Adderley, 'in spite of outstanding gifts and aristocratic connections, he remained humble and unaffected; he retained something of that childlikeness such as our Lord demanded of His disciples'. It would seem that the shared qualities of humility and piety served to draw Adderley and Woodward together, as did the 'mutual affection' which they felt for one another. This 'mutual affection' was remembered by the organist at St Mark's, Francis Burgess, who was himself a significant figure in the contemporary revival of Plainsong. He too had served at the Berkeley Chapel, and was appointed to St Mark's in 1902.

Adderley described St Mark's as being 'a small parish of poor people surrounded by the rich and intellectual'.[2] He was concerned to give the people full Anglo-catholic ritual, including the use of incense, and the main Sunday service was a Sung Eucharist at 10.00 am. He also wished to stimulate their minds, and to that end the Sunday eucharist was followed by a lecture. In his recollections *In Slums and Society* Adderley wrote with obvious pride about the intellectual calibre of the men he persuaded to deliver these 'lectures on critical questions', thinkers and scholars of the quality of Scott Holland, Driver, Sanday, and Inge. He also recalled how Woodward disapproved of some of the teaching which the lectures contained, writing 'Some "rather hot" doctrines were occasionally put forth from the pulpit, and I remember how my assistant priest, one of the old school (Revd G. R. Woodward of Plainsong fame), used to sit in the sedilia fuming over the lectures and muttering the Athanasian Creed as a relief to his feelings.'[3] One particular incident was recalled by Burgess, who wrote 'On one occasion when the late Dr F. W. Cobb preached at St Mark's, giving St John's Gospel a latish date, Woodward concluded the service by praying "Give us grace, that, being not like children carried away with every blast of vain doctrine, we may be established in the truth of Thy Holy Gospel."'[4]

When Adderley left St Mark's in 1904, it would not have seemed a good moment for Woodward to begin any new parochial commitment, for the remarkable hymnal *Songs of Syon* which he edited – and which, in view of the fact that he translated or composed many of the words, and harmonised a number of the tunes, he rather more than just edited – was about to make its first appearance, and since this collection continued to grow and evolve over the next four years, it must have continued to occupy much of his time. In not being published in its entirety at the first instance, *Songs of Syon* followed the pattern of *The Cowley Carol Book*, and indeed of Woodward's first *Carols for Christmas-tide* ten years earlier. In 1904 the words and tunes for the first edition of *Songs of Syon* appeared separately, the tunes, in an oblong format suitable for the organ loft, being published by Messrs Schott & Co., whilst the words were published by the Plainsong and Mediaeval Music Society and printed by the sisters at Wantage. The items included numbered to two hundred and one, and the full title for this first edition was *Songs of Syon: A Collection of Hymns & Sacred Poems Mostly Translated from Ancient Greek, Latin and German Sources.* For this first edition, the Preface was written by Athelstan Riley, although both the content and the style of it suggest that Woodward himself played a part in its composition. Once more the question of language arises, and the writer states:

> In some of the hymns a few archaic words and phrases appear. Those who are aquainted with the Editor's former poems and translations will recognise an individuality of style which we expect in all that comes from his pen. Apart from this, not only does there seem a certain artistic propriety in setting melodies of the XVIth and XVIIth centuries to words in the style of the period, but it is surely better to employ the English of King James' Bible and the Book of Common Prayer, with which the hymns are intended to be used, than that colloquial English which is wanting in the solemnity which in all human affairs, springs spontaneously from the associations of the past.[5]

Another part of the Preface which seems to have a distinct flavour of Woodward's own thought and writing is this:

> The hymns selected or specially provided will be found Catholick and objective, definite and dogmatic; and whilst a few are more suitable for private than for public use as being of a personal and fervid character, the sentimental doggerel, which disfigures even the best of our modern hymn-books, has been rigorously excluded. No attempt has been made to dilute the Faith – the book is intended for instructed, Church-people, not for the half-converted ...[6]

Woodward continued to work on the collection, and in 1908 a third and considerably enlarged edition was published, bearing the amended title *Songs of Syon: A Collection of Psalms, Hymns, and Spiritual Songs for Public and Private Use.* It contained four hundred and thirty-one

items. Music and words continued to appear separately, with
a slip of paper in the words edition reading 'A Tune-Book
corresponding with this Edition is in the course of preparation. But, so long as the demand continues, copies of the
previous editions of "Songs of Syon" may still be procured of
Messrs Schott: Music, 5s; words only 1s, net.' For this third
edition of 1908, Athelstan Riley's Preface was abandoned,
and replaced by a brief Preface written by Woodward
himself. Finally in 1910 the Third Edition was republished
with the words and music being united in one volume for the
first time, and with Woodward providing a new and greatly
extended Preface. The 1908 words edition had been very
attractively produced, being illustrated by woodcuts
pertaining to the various feasts and seasons of the Church's
Year, and artistically the 1910 volume was a worthy
successor. The publisher was again Messrs Schott & Co, and
Dr Watkins Shaw has commented on the firm's courage in
taking on a project of which the commercial success must
have been questionable from the very outset. Even a cursory
glance at *Songs of Syon*, however, reveals it to be an impressive achievement, a work which the anonymous writer of
Woodward's obituary in the *Church Times* declared to be
'the finest hymn book, both as regards words and music, ever
produced in England',[7] whilst Kenneth Long in his book *The
Music of the English Church* called it 'a monument of careful
scholarship, wide culture, and sensitive imagination'.[8]
Woodward's two closest friends and collaborators, Charles
Wood and G. H. Palmer, were both closely associated with
the work, and it is dedicated to the latter, who, the 1910
Preface observes, 'freely bestowed an immense amount of
time, thought, labour, and trouble in the preparation of this
Work, in reading and revising proofs of the letter-press, as
well as of the music-note, besides harmonizing a very considerable number of tunes'.[9]

As in his other collections, the Preface which Woodward
wrote for the 1910 edition makes illuminating reading, and
three characteristics which are found there seem particularly
significant. First, there is a vigorous and perhaps to some a
surprising practicality about his approach. It is true that
Woodward was aiming to produce a hymnal in which the

very finest tunes would be collected together, and in which there would be no place for anything which was not in itself excellent; he had no intention of making any concession whatsoever to popular taste – which is largely why, of course, the book has never come into anything like general use. But despite this disdain for the merely popular, he clearly hoped that *Songs of Syon* would be widely used, and consequently he provided very practical and detailed directions about performance. Regarding Plainsong, for example, he wrote:

> The Plainsong Melodies must be sung *lightly* and *quasi loquendo*, with due attention to the tonal accents ... On no account should they be *dragged*; on no account *hurried*. The pace will depend, to some extent, on the accoustic properties of the building, the size of the Quire, the volume of the sound proceeding from the lips of the congregation; but the right *tempo* must be determined by the style of the Melody and the character of the harmony. The more elaborate settings, especially those of Bach, require slower singing than the simple ones. The Quire-master will be guided herein by his own musical intuition and good taste.[10]

All this is certainly very practical, and yet in the final sentence – as in an appended note to this paragraph urging regular congregational choir practices – there is possibly a certain degree of unrealistic and hence misplaced optimism. Then a second characteristic of Woodward's approach as found in the Preface is that refusal to compromise which has already been alluded to. He wrote, for example,

> Concerning the Style of the Harmonies. It is frankly avowed that these are mostly old-fashioned. With a bold disregard for later conventionalities, the harmonies of each earlier age have been retained. That which may sound as a 'false relation' to modern ears was not disagreeable to the taste of our musical forefathers ... To have harmonized 'Agincourt' c.1415, for instance, in the style of 1910, would have been an anachronism, and in every instance it is hoped that this fault has been guarded against.[11]

No concessions; the pursuit of the excellent and the correct; the veneration which the conservative feels for the practice of a bygone age: all, it might be argued, providing an accurate expression of Woodward's own outlook and personality. But if that is so, it is completed by a third characteristic – or at least a striking and unusual note – which is found in the 1910 Preface, namely Woodward's genuine and old-world piety. Few Prefaces, even to religious books, end as this one does: 'Lastly, the Editor asks the singers and readers of *Songs of Syon*, of their charity, to remember him sometimes in their prayers during his life-time, and to bid for the repose of his soul after death.' This piety, and that real humility which those who knew him all remarked upon, are seen too in his placing the following inscription at the end of the hymnal:

*Memento Mei, Deus Meus, Pro Hoc; et Parce*
*Mihi Secundum Multitudium*
*Miserationem*
*Tuarum*[12]

The fact that Woodward was ready in *Songs of Syon*, as in *The Cowley Carol Book*, to write words for tunes which he considered good but which did not already have suitable words attached to them, indicates that in compiling his hymnal it was again the music to which he gave the primary place, a practice which is perhaps even more questionable in the case of hymns that it is in the case of carols. It may be argued that in a hymnal both words and music should be given at least equal weight. Here, the fact that good tunes seem to have been the first concern means that many outstanding sets of words do not appear; only one hymn each by Charles Wesley and George Herbert, for example, find inclusion. The tunes fall, according to the Preface, into five categories: Plainsong Melodies, Metrical Melodies of the 13th to the 16th Centuries, Lutheran Tunes, Old English and Scotch Psalm-Tunes of the 16th and 17th Centuries, and old French Psalm-Tunes and Canticles of the Sixteenth Century. The inclusion of two tunes composed by Charles Wood and four by Wagner seem, almost incredibly, to be practically the only concession not just to Woodward's own generation of composers, but to those of the two preceding centuries. Whilst many of the harmonisations date from the sixteenth and seventeenth centuries, a considerable number are modern, Woodward himself having written around fifty of them, whilst Wood and Palmer each contributed about thirty.

It comes as no surprise to find that a great number of the words in *Songs of Syon* come from the pen of J. M. Neale; there are, in fact, no less than one hundred and twenty items of his, mostly translations of ancient Greek and Latin hymns. But even more were written by Woodward himself – one hundred and forty translations and twenty new compositions. The Preface contains a similar explanation-cum-apology for this to the one given in *The Cowley Carol Book*: he writes again of the peculiar metre of some of the tunes, and of how English hymn-writers and translators 'decline to be trammelled' with their 'uncommon measures'. He recalls how the use of existing words has sometimes led to the foreign melody being 'mutilated' and states that he has:

> discovered long ago that where there were no words available in the exact measure of certain tunes which he wished to make better known, he had no alternative but to provide words of his own. This must be his apology for the frequent recurrence of his own initials. But where English Hymn-writers or Translators had already provided suitable words *in the right metre* for some particular tune, he was only too thankful to make use of their labours and publish their verses.[13]

Here again the primacy which Woodward gave to the music is evident, and also his exacting standards concerning the precise metrical unity which should exist between words and music. This last led to the inclusion of an unusually detailed metrical index in *Songs of Syon*. The range of 'other' writers and translators who fulfilled Woodward's criteria is somewhat limited: they include W. J. Blew (1808–1894), over twenty of whose translations are included, F. W. Faber (1814–1863), several of whose original compositions are used, and Robert Bridges (1844–1930), the Poet Laureate. Bridges had produced his own hymn book, the *Yattendon Hymnal* in 1898, and Woodward took six sets of words from it. In the Preface to *Songs of Syon* he stated that 'To Mr Robert Bridges belongs the credit ... of being the first to provide English words, in the right metre, for many of L. Bourgeois' finest melodies', and he kept a letter which Bridges wrote to him on the publication of *Songs of Syon* in 1904, which began 'I congratulate you on getting out your book and thank you for sending me copies. It is very pleasantly printed. I am glad that you have thought any thing of mine worthy to go into it, and am particularly pleased at heading the Evening hymns with *Phos Hilaron*.'[14]

In the main the verses which Woodward himself composed for *Songs of Syon*, or translated from the Greek, Latin, or German, are not outstanding. Perhaps the sheer number of the tunes for which he set himself to provide words meant that his inspiration could not be other than thinly spread. Maybe one of the more successful free translations which he made is that for J. Franck's well-known eucharistic hymn, which begins:

> Deck thee, O my soul, with gladness,
> Quit thy haunts of sin and sadness;
> Like the dying thief forgiven,
> And with sinful Mary shriven,
> Thou must go, as saith the Psalter,
> To thy God and to his Altar:
> Heed the word by Jesus spoken,
> 'Take and eat my Body broken',[15]

Although this translation has been eclipsed in popular use by the arguably more bland one made by Catherine Winkworth (1827–1878) – several of whose translations Woodward includes in *Songs of Syon* – it deserves to be known and used. The same thing has happened with his translation of 'O *Esca Viatorum*', the rather similar translation made by his friend Athelstan Riley having been generally preferred. However in the case of '*Leibster Jesu*', Woodward's very satisfactory translation has continued in use through its inclusion in *Hymns Ancient and Modern*. Again his straightforward and unaffected translation of Petrus Herbert's evening hymn is successful. It begins:

> Now it is evening; time to cease from labour,
> Father, according to thy will and pleasure,
> Through the night season, have thy faithful people
> Safe in thy keeping.[16]

This has come to be widely known and used in recent years through its inclusion in *The Divine Office* of the Catholic Church.

Whilst some of Woodward's new compositions for *Songs of Syon* are not perhaps so successful as his translations, there is occasionally some striking – if somewhat over-lush – imagery to be found, as in the hymn 'Life is Full of Trouble', one of those hymns which would certainly appear to have been written to match an unusual metre. The first verse reads:

> Life is full of trouble;
>     Fleet as foam before the wind,
> Frail as water-bubble,
>         E'en as clover,
>         Summer over,
> Wither'd grass and stubble.
> Noting time on dial,
>     Death with bony hand doth break
> Gilt and crystal vial:
>         Or will shatter
>         Earthen platter,
> Brooking no denial.
> Through town, o'er down and dale,
>     Or where the ocean surges,
> Grim death his palfrey pale
>         Daily, nightly urges:
>         In his rear
>         Knells I hear
> Requiems and dirges.[17]

As another example of the new compositions made for *Songs of Syon*, his carol 'There is a Plant' is worth quoting. It has considerable charm, and demonstrates how pleasing his verses can be:

> There is a plant of noble form and hue,
>     From Paradise it came, this royal flower,
> Born of the breath of God and morning dew,
>     Nurtur'd and water'd of the heav'nly shower:
> Mid thorns and thistle lily'like it grew,
>     And oped at Christmas in my Lady's bower.
>
> A white and ruddy Rose, with rich perfume,
>     As balsam sweet, unto the mouth as honey:
> 'Tis ay in blossom, in December's gloom,
>     As in July, on cloudy days or sunny:
> Way-faring men may cull this priceless Bloom,
>     An so they will, for love, and free of money.

Jesu, thou art this Rose, of Jesse's stem,
   The Virgin-born, whose praise my song engages:
O for the heav'nly new Hierusalem,
   Land, free from summer's heat and winter's rages,
Where I might eye thee, Babe of Bethlehem,
   And chaunt thy grace through never-ending ages! [18]

In seeking to estimate the success of *Songs of Syon* it is necessary to ask whether or not Woodward was seeking to
produce a hymnal which was complete in itself, or just a
supplement to be used alongside other more comprehensive
hymn books. If the latter, then of course the criticism that
some of the finest sets of words ever written are excluded,
together with many well-loved tunes, falls to the ground,
since these could be found in other, existing hymnals.
Quoting from the preface to the 1904 edition, C. S. Phillips
points out that it was originally intended 'not to compete
with existing hymnals, but only to supplement them'.[19]
Those words, however, were written by Riley, not by
Woodward, even though the latter must have given his
approval. Yet it is significant that nothing is said about *Songs
of Syon* being merely a supplement in the 1908 and 1910
Prefaces, and the contents of the enlarged third edition,
which provide hymns for all the seasons and feasts of the
Church's Year, together with a large selection of general
hymns, carols, metrical psalms, and spiritual songs, suggests
that the editor had a more ambitious intention, namely the
production of what he considered to be the ideal hymnal. A
hymnal which in Dom Anslem Hughes' words had been
compiled 'without the slightest concession to popular taste
and containing only the best of hymns and tunes according
to the judgement of the compiler'.[20] Thirty years after the
first appearance of *Songs of Syon*, the writer of Woodward's
obituary in the *Church Times* (already referred to) sought to
provide a brief evaluation of the book, and having called it
'the finest book, as regards words and music, ever produced
in England', continued 'allowing, of course, for the limitation that practically all modern music was excluded from the
book ... It is seldom that so much poetic and musical taste
have been combined in the same person'. It does indeed have
to be admitted that the limitations of *Songs of Syon* are as

obvious as its excellence, and in this it is a kind of microcosm of Woodward himself. The labour, scholarship, strength of purpose, and the love of excellence which underlie the hymnal continue to amaze; as the writer of a Tribute in the *Eastern Daily Press* said at the time of Woodward's death, 'it was a tremendous task to collect and edit some five hundred of the world's best tunes, and in many cases write the words to fit them',[21] and yet the limitations which Woodward imposed upon himself are all too apparent. Athelstan Riley in his memoir claimed that it was the 'archaism of the language which prevented *Songs of Syon* becoming a popular hymn-book', but this is only part of the reason why few places of worship ever used the book, despite the acclamation which it has continued to receive from church musicians. Rather it was the exclusion of all material which did not meet Woodward's exacting and particular standards, including fine words which had no fine tune to fit them, which effectively prevented it from finding acceptance as a standard hymn book. For if on the one hand its being largely produced by a single editor meant that the book 'had the supreme advantage that the choice of both words and music came from the same mind',[22] it also meant that there was inevitably a certain narrowness of sympathy, appreciation, and judgement, particularly when the single editor in question had tastes which, whilst excellent, were also limited. Perhaps the fact that those who have shared his fastidious tastes have continued to applaud the book would have meant more to Woodward than its passing into general use; certainly Riley seems to have been correct in saying that 'popularity was the last thing Woodward ever sought', and the fact that its appeal has proved to be so limited would not have surprised him greatly. His aim was excellence rather than commercial success, and within the limited parameters which he set himself, this aim was undoubtedly achieved.

Between the first edition of *Songs of Syon* in 1904 and its appearance in its final form in 1910, another hymnal was published which was to achieve a success to which *Songs of Syon* never did, and, for the reasons just suggested, perhaps never could, attain. This was *The English Hymnal*, the first edition of which appeared in 1906. Since the General Editor was Percy Dearmer (1867–1936), with whom Woodward had worked briefly at the Berkeley Chapel, and the Musical Editor was Ralph Vaughan Williams (1872–1958), who had spent a short time as Organist at St Barnabas' Pimlico, it was hardly surprising that Woodward should have been invited to serve on the committee for the new hymnal, especially in view of the reputation which he had achieved as editor both of the successful *Cowley Carol Book* and the impressive *Songs of Syon*. All did not go well for Woodward, however, and according to the so-far unidentified 'H. A. K.' who wrote the 'Appreciation' of Woodward in the *Eastern Daily Press* following his death in 1934, he 'fell out' from the committee. Mervyn Horder asserts that this resignation was due to the fact that he could not accept the inclusion of a hymn having words written by someone who was not a confessing Christian, the particular writer being William Blake, and the words being those of the poem 'To Mercy, Pity, Peace and Love'.[23] Mervyn Horder recalls having been told this by the late Cyril Taylor, who also expressed the opinion that Woodward initially enjoyed working on the committee, which included his friends W. J. Birkbeck and Athelstan Riley, and felt quite deeply the sacrifice which his conscience caused him to make. The disagreement might explain why none of Woodward's work appears in either *The English Hymnal* or in *The Oxford Book of Carols*, the latter being edited by Dearmer in 1928. It also provides a telling insight into Woodward's strict adherence to his principles, an adherence which might variously be judged as courageous or as merely narrow, but which certainly speaks of a rigorous integrity.

The year 1910 saw not only the publication of *Songs of Syon* in its final form, but also the appearance of another of Woodward's major works. This was the edition of *Piae Cantiones* which he prepared for the Plainsong and Mediaeval Music Society. *Piae Cantiones* is a remarkable collection of seventy-four Latin hymns and school songs collected by Theodoric Petri of Nyland, a Finn, and published in 1582. As Woodward wrote in the Preface to this edition, Petri had set himself 'to rescue and preserve for future use some of the most beautiful psalms, hymns, and school songs for the Mediaeval church in Finland', and the book which he produced continued to be used throughout the Swedish lands well into the eighteenth century. In praising Petri's collection, Woodward seems to be indicating his own ideals when he writes 'The whole book is possessed of a healthy tone, of a religious, chivalrous spirit, with an elevating influence, and is interesting if only because it sets forth the then accepted standards of all that was good, noble, and beautiful in ordinary daily life'.[24]

Two things about Woodward's edition strike the reader immediately. First, what a finely-produced volume it is. Printed for the Plainsong and Mediaeval Music Society by the Chiswick Press, the type-face and layout together with the paper and binding are all of the highest standard. According to Dom Anslem Hughes the music-type of the 1582 edition was reproduced by means of line-blocks taken from drawings made by Woodward himself; Hughes recalled that 'so well was this done that I have been asked "Where did the Chiswick Press get their type from?" '[25] The second thing which immediately impresses the reader is the vast scholarship which is evidenced both in the lengthy Preface and in the even fuller Notes at the back of the book. Woodward's knowledge of both the theory and history of the music, and of the history and use of the Latin texts which accompany it, is clearly the fruit of prolonged and meticulous research, and in this the reason why he was unable to undertake regular parochial duties after 1904 becomes readily apparent. In his memoir, Riley speaks of Woodward relinquishing parish work and of 'devoting himself to literary and musical studies', spending much of his time in the Reading Room of the British Museum. Perhaps the considerable learning which resulted from his researches it seen most clearly in the Preface and Notes which accompany *Piae Cantiones*.

In the Preface to this edition, as is in the Preface to *Songs of Syon*, an approach is seen which is practical rather than archeological; it is clear that Woodward hopes that the book will be used in worship. Whilst a mere facsimile of the 1582 edition would, he writes, have 'satisfied musicians, scholars, and antiquarians', it would not have been 'of any practical use, and possible "in Quires and Places where they sing" '. It

G. R. Woodward playing the euphonium outside Walsingham
Vicarage in the eighteen-eighties.

## The Mother of my Lord

I   *Gabriel, of high degree.*

Gabriel, of high degree,
  Cometh from the Trinitie,
    On our Lady-day in Lent:
Nazareth, of Galilee,
  Is the city, whither he,
    Loaden with good news, is ſent.

He met a Maiden in that place,
  And fell down before her face,
    Singing, 'Hail! Thou Virgin mild;
Hail! Saint Mary, full of grace:
  Fear not; bliſsful is thy caſe:
    Jeſus Chriſt will be thy Child.'
Quoth the Maid, 'How ſhall it be,
  How ſhall babe be born of me,
    Seeing that I know not man?'

(3)

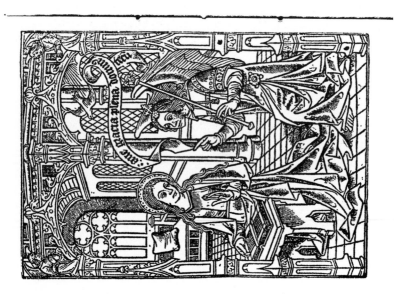

THE MOTHER OF MY LORD OR CAROLS FOR OUR LADY,
written by G. R. Woodward, and printed by him at Highgate

would be easy to see – and indeed to dismiss – Woodward
with his copious and learned notes, and, here again in *Piae
Cantiones*, with his archaic 'long S', as belonging simply to
the camp of 'musicians, scholars, and antiquarians'. But that
would be to misunderstand and indeed to underestimate
him. He was always concerned with the performance of
hymns and carols, which he saw himself as making available
for ordinary use. Another of Woodward's concerns which
comes out clearly in the Preface is that strong and uncompromising approach to theological orthodoxy which has
already been evidenced by his muttering the Athanasian
Creed during the 'rather hot' lectures at St Mark's. He claims
that a 'principal hindrance' to the production of a facsimile
copy of *Piae Cantiones* was the possible 'introduction and
toleration of grave doctrinal errors' which might result from
the words of the 1582 edition being reprinted just as they
stood. In various cases the mediaeval words had been altered
by Petri and maybe others to conform with the opinions of
the late-sixteenth-century Lutheran Church in Sweden, and
altered Woodward states 'not for the better but for the
worse'. These changes had occurred, he asserts, 'chiefly in
regard to certain expressions of their devotion to her whom
all generations shall call Blessed', and he sternly observes
with regard to the mediaeval writers that the compilers
should 'have left their writings alone'. Only, he contends, if
the Latin words are returned to their original, unexpurgated
form will it be right to use them again.

It would be surprising if J. M. Neale was not somewhere in
the background of Woodward's work with *Piae Cantiones*,
and in the Preface he relates that the very rare copy which he
had used for his new edition had once belonged to Neale. It
had been brought to England by a former British envoy and
minister at Stockholm, given by him to Neale, bequeathed by
Neale to Helmore, and bought from Helmore's son by the
Plainsong and Mediaeval Music Society. Woodward speaks
of Neale's high regard for the book, and of the use he made
of it in preparing, with Helmore, his *Carols for Christmas-
tide* in 1853 and its sequel *Carols for Easter-tide* in 1854. But
Woodward is not uncritical of Neale's use of the book in
those earlier works, for whilst he greatly admired and rever-

enced his 'master', he was an independently-minded scholar and no blind hero-worshipper. In his note on *In Hoc Anno Circulo*, for example, he explains that the rule as to the interpretation of the 'ligature' was not clearly understood when Neale and Helmore's collections were published, and that 'in many other instances also, the tunes of *Piae Cantiones* have been, unintentionally but nevertheless incorrectly transcribed in Neale and Helmore's otherwise admirable work'.[26]

Throughout the first decade of the new century Woodward clearly toiled intensively, producing in those relatively few years his three major works, *The Cowley Carol Book, First Series*, in 1901/1902, *Songs of Syon* between 1904 and 1910, and his edition of *Piae Cantiones* in 1910. After all of this he may have felt the need of some literary light-relief, and he seems to have found this in the writing of *Cock Robin and Jenny Wren. A Ballad for Children*, which was published in 1911. This is in the form of a booklet, bound in paper, and printed simply but well at the Chiswick Press. It is dedicated to his niece Rhoda Margaret Clarke, who was presumably a daughter of his sister Helen. The fact that it claims to be written for children does not prevent it from having some rather scholarly Explanatory Notes appended to it, and it is hardly a forerunner of the modern children's book. The Ballad, made up of forty six-line indented verses, is not without charm, and perhaps on account of its form it flows more easily than some of the long narrative poems, written in couplets and not broken up into verses, which he more usually wrote. It describes the marriage of Cock Robin and Jenny Wren, and despite the fact that it mainly concerns itself with describing the birds which attended their nuptials, he manages – rather wittily – to introduce bees:

> In prospect of glad Honey-moon,
> Came swarms of Bees that afternoon;
> And, as the day was sunny,
> In ample time they did arrive,
> And bore a comb-ful from the hive;
> Far sweeter thing than money.[27]

It is interesting that Woodward describes himself on the title-page as 'Sometime Vicar of Little Walsingham', and in the course of describing the guests at the wedding he writes:

And there the hungry Cormoraunt
And Storm-cock, that had left his haunt
　　At End-of-Land, or New-Quay:
And Hernshaw, bred below the dam
And Wishing-well at Walsingham,
　　Beside the banks of Stewkey.[28]

The banks of Stewkey – written Stiffkey – the Wishing-well,
the Hernshaw (or heron), and the dam (the latter to be swept
away in a disastrous flood in the following year, 1912) were
all to be found in the grounds of the Lee Warner home, The
Abbey, Walsingham. Woodward's affection for Walsingham
seems to have continued, and this was not the last publication in which he would place the name of his former parish
after his own.

Not, however, that *Cock Robin and Jenny Wren* was his
only publication in 1911, for a substantial volume of verse
also appeared in that year called *Golden Lays of Olden
Days*, being, he wrote, 'Twenty various pieces, mostly based
upon ancient Hebrew, Greek, Latin and German originals
(poetry and prose) drawn into English rime'. Again, as in
certain other Prefaces, he reveals something of his own principles and preferences in the way in which he introduces the
collection, writing 'some of the Lays are printed, not so
much for their literary value or historical exactitude, as for
their quaint old-world simplicity and directness; and none
but men of a proud spirit, and of an irreverent and unbelieving frame of mind, will presume to think scorn of these
strange compositions, bearing as they do, evident marks of
the honest faith, and child-like piety of their now unknown
writers'.[29] We see here an expression of Woodward's liking
for 'simplicity and directness', a simplicity which is seen in
the terse phrases which characterise most of his carols, and in
the directness of expression which is found in his Prefaces
and in his few remaining sermons. We also see, however, an
intolerance for those who do not share his views, and a
readiness to condemn them as proud, irreverent and
unbelieving, and yet alongside this there is a more endearing
love of piety and devotion, and an attraction to the 'quaint'
and 'old-world'. It was of course his preference for quaint
and old-world language which has so often led to his being

criticised, and indeed not being taken seriously, and it will be
remembered that Athelstan Riley considered this to have
been the main factor which prevented the wide use of *Songs
of Syon*. Woodward seems to have been fully aware of this
criticism, and very sensitive to it. Although he would allude
to the matter in his Preface to *The Cowley Carol Book,
Second Series*, in 1919, it was here in the preface to *Golden
Lays of Olden Days* that he made his most full and most
robust defence of the practice, writing:

> The author has again deliberately laid himself open to the
> charge of 'affecting obsolete words' and employing an 'archaic
> manner of speech' ... But it is not from false 'affectation' but
> rather genuine 'affection' for ancient poets that he writes in an
> old-fashioned style; and, sooth to say, by much reading and
> admiration of their works, somehow unconsciously he has
> assimilated and made their thoughts and diction his very own.
> For this use of archaisms he is content to be blamed, and to go
> wrong in the good company of Vergil, Chaucer, Gawain,
> Chatterton and others who were all notorious offenders in
> this matter. But he hopes to be forgiven by his kind and
> courteous criticks and readers, for still having the bad taste
> to prefer the English of the writers of the Elizabethan age
> rather than that of the present date, and he craves pardon for
> trying to recover and retain some of the simple language and
> homely phrases once on the lips of his pious Anglo-Saxon
> forefathers.[30]

Courteous and uncompromising, intractable and yet with
humour not far away, this is Woodward at his most typical
and at his best. The pages which follow the Preface
contain verse translations from the Apocrypha, and then a
selection of legends of the Saints – always a favourite subject
for Woodward – in which figures as diverse as St Agnes,
St Barbara, St Caedmon and St Edward the Confessor are
met with. Again, it is interesting to discover from the
Preface that his approach to the Saints had that same
practical aspect as is evident in his approach to hymns and
carols; he wanted the latter to be performed in normal
worship, and the former to be imitated in daily life: 'Should
the author ... stir up only two or three of his gentle
readers to take fresh interest in the Lives of the Saints, and to
follow them, as they were followers of the Lord (*utinam*

*Deus ita faxit!*), then his labour will not altogether have been spent in vain'.[31]

Meanwhile his interest in Plainsong continued unabated, doubtless encouraged by his membership of the Council of the Plainsong and Mediaeval Music Society from 1904 onwards and his close association with Francis Burgess between 1901 and 1904 at St Mark's Marylebone. James Adderley described him as being 'of plainsong fame', which certainly suggests his continuing enthusiasm, as does the inclusion of many plainsong melodies in *Songs of Syon*. Typically firm principles were applied to those melodies: no harmonies were provided for them 'it being the Editor's firm conviction that unless the organist be a well-instructed and sympathetic Church musician, Gregorian music is better when sung without instrumental accompaniment'.[32] In 1912, and in company with E. M. Goldsmith, he prepared for publication – again by the Plainsong and Mediaeval Music Society – *Fourteen Ancient Fauxbourdons (Magnificat)*.

Finally as regards his publications during the period 1901 to 1916, there were three books of translations from ancient texts. The first, in 1912, was *Cupid and Psyche. From the Latin of Apuleis. Done into English Verse in Nine Cantos.* This was 'gratefully dedicated to my scholarly and courteous friend Arthur Isaac Ellis M.A. Assistant Librarian, British Museum', a dedication which may be an acknowledgement of the assistance which he had received in the Museum Reading Room during the previous few years. Then in 1913 and 1914 he published two translations from the Greek, *St John of Damascus. Canon for the Repose of The Mother of God,* and *St John Damascene. Balaam and Joasaph*, the latter appearing in the Loeb Classical Library series. *Cupid and Psyche* is significant in that it is the first of a number of translations from Classical literature made in the last twenty years of his life, rather as if he was beginning to look back to the time when he had been a Classical Scholar at Cambridge. The other two translations, of works by a Greek father, also mark the beginning of a new interest, insofar as they are the first of several translations from the literature of the Greek Church which would appear over the

next few years. The verse translation of St John of Damascus'
*Canon for the Repose of The Mother of God* was little
more than a pamphlet, being a re-print from the *Dublin
Review*, but the prose translation of the same writers
*Balaam and Joasaph*, made jointly with H. Mattingly, fellow
of his old college Gonville and Caius, was a much more
considerable undertaking, the printed book having over six
hundred pages, with the Greek text on one page and the
English translation given opposite to it. Significantly the
translation is not made in contemporary English: the
Preface explains that 'the whole work is steeped in the
language of the Bible and of the Church Fathers; and it is
this fact which has led the translators to adopt a style
modelled on that of the Authorised Version'.[33] Perhaps
this is just indicative of the period in which the translation was made, but maybe it also illustrates Woodward's
very conservative, Anglican, and ecclesiastical approach to
his work.

During these years Woodward was in regular correspon-
dence with his half-sister Annie, and a dozen or so of her
letters to him survive, the earliest of these, according to the
postmark on the envelope, having been written in 1905.[34] It
seems that her second husband, the Revd W. F. Eaton, was
dead by this time, and that she lived in rooms or hotels, often
accompanied by her son Claude. Most summers were spent
in Germany, at Bad Nanheim, where she took the cure and
which she refers to as 'my beloved Nanheim', although it
seems that there were also regular visits to Italy. In England
she favoured hotels in London and Eastbourne, although in
a letter from Eastbourne written in 1909 she wrote 'we
move into our nice old rooms next Saturday ... Hotels are
impossible with their cheap food and vile cooking at ruinous
prices'. Like his half-sister, Woodward was also living in
hotels at this time, and it appears that he too may have made
visits to the continent: writing from Bad Nanheim on one
occasion Annie says 'could you not manage a few days here
on your way to Bavaria or back? How you must long for the
change after London, which seems to grow more terrible
every year, with its heat & turmoil & restlessness'. Apart
from this reference, the only other surviving indication of

Woodward's having travelled abroad – other than his cycling to Rome as a young man – is the fact that the Preface to revised edition of *The Cowley Carol Book, First Series* is dated 'Cadenabbia, Oct. 24th 1902'. Cadenabbia is on the shores of Lake Como.

Like her half-brother, Annie was a staunch Conservative, and strongly anti-Liberal. Their common political outlook led her to remark in one letter 'Yes, dear George, I think you & I are the only *true* descendants of our good Father, & feel as he did'. King George V found immediate favour with her, and she wrote at the time of his accession:

> I hear all good of King George, he is a strong Conservative, *very* firm and determined, & it is believed he will not let these traitors play the fool. I hear he has already put Asquith in his place: that the police have intimated to L. George they cannot be responsible for his safely & that craven Mr Churchill was hissed by his own yeomanry. May it all be true & much more to come!

Like so many of their class and background in pre-First World War days, the brother and half-sister were enthusiastic about Germany and German culture, an enthusiasm which Annie expressed with characteristic vigour in another of her letters:

> I just love the Germans, a <u>fine</u> race, they are <u>very</u> near the spiritual world. One can feel no wonder they produced a Goëthe, a Bach, & above all a Wagner! How <u>proud</u> they must be to belong to such a people. I feel so at home with all these dear people, they look at you with their Souls. We flee before the English, who are so dull, unfeeling, stupid, nothing but <u>shallow</u> talk! I always hope if ever my Claude marries, it will be to a German or Austrian, they put all English silly young women to shame ...'

Woodward can hardly have agreed with the preference of Wagner to Bach, despite his sharing of her liking for the former; on one occasion Annie thanked him for sending her 'that delicious book on Parsifal', perhaps *Wagner's Parsifal* written by Alfred Gurney.

But if Woodward and his half-sister were both like their father in espousing strong Tory views, it was only Annie who shared in his equally strong anti-Catholic opinions. With her

own very individualistic religious approach, largely made up
of some general ethical principles wedded to sentiment, she
wrote in one of her letters:

> Until we have thrown away all rites and doctrines & sought &
> found God, Each person for themselves, then only does he live
> and soar into the heavenly Presences. Believe me, dear George,
> I am right & know by great Experience that I am right. Seek
> Him only & 'He will guide us with His eye', not like horse &
> mule which have no understanding & must be held with bit
> & bridle by the Church, & terribly ignorant bad drivers,
> the clergy. I am only waiting until you can see as I do. It
> must come.

There is no evidence that it did, and his half-sister's dislike of
his religious opinions seem to have had no more effect upon
him than that of his father.

Because Annie largely confines herself in these letters to
accounts of her movements and of her political and religious
opinions, comparatively little can be learned from them
either about Woodward himself or about other members of
the family. The fact that she enquires about Nellie (Helen)
suggests that Woodward was in regular contact with his
sister at this time, and there are regular expressions of sorrow
and alarm concerning Basil's health. Annie clearly disapproved of Basil's marriage; in one letter, having spoken of
some notably devoted wife, she adds 'Oh! Why, Why, had
not Basil common sense? but I suppose the cry "We choose
Barabbas" will always be the same from all those ages down-
wards'. Basil died in 1914, and since a letter from his widow
– inviting Woodward to conduct the funeral service – is
signed 'Milly', it may be her to whom Annie refers in an
earlier letter as 'that extraordinary little Milly' and as a 'sly
little minx'.

After leaving Alderney Street in the early years of the
century, Woodward lived at 7 Shelley Court, Tite Street,
Chelsea. He was there in 1905, but by 1908 he had moved to
the Eccleston Square Hotel, and in the following year he was
living at The Ivanhoe Hotel, Bloomsbury Street, which was
conveniently near to the British Museum Reading Room.
According to addresses on envelopes and his entries in
*Crockford's Clerical Directory*, he remained there until 1916

when, tired perhaps with hotel life, and with his main researchers completed, he began to rent a house in North London. He was sixty-eight when he settled in Highgate, and it was there that he would spend the remaining eighteen years of his life.

CHAPTER SEVEN

# HIGHGATE 1916–1924

The eighteenth-century architect Robert Adam wrote of the 'mountainous village of Highgate', claiming that it and its neighbour Hampstead formed 'delightful objects' in the landscape.[1] Set on a ridge rising to four hundred feet above the Thames, Highgate still retained an essentially rural air at the beginning of the present century, and according to one description, 'though Highgate stood in a wilderness of suburbs, it had the air of a Middlesex village'.[2] From 1916 Woodward rented 48 West Hill (it was renumbered 81 in 1939), buying the property in about 1919.[3] A spacious house, probably dating from the early years of the nine-teenth-century, it is plain, square, stuccoed and set back from the pavement behind a wall, through which a doorway leads into a small entrance courtyard. There is a garden behind the house, on land which falls away steeply. The house is almost at the top of West Hill, which remains a pleasant if fairly busy thoroughfare, in parts still overhung by trees.[4] Living a little way down West Hill at number 31, and aged ten when Woodward moved there in 1916, was the future Poet Laureate John Betjeman. He powerfully evokes the place and the period in his verse-autobiography *Summoned by Bells*, writing:

> Deeply I loved thee, 31 West Hill!
> At that hills' foot did London then begin,
> With yellow horse-trams clopping past the planes
> To grey-brick nonconformist Chetwynd Road
> And on to Kentish Town and barking dogs
> And costers' carts and crowded grocers' shops
> And Daniels' store, the local Selfridges,
> The Bon Marche, the Electric Palace, slums
> That thrilled me with their smells of poverty –
> Till, safe once more, we gained the leafy slope
> And buttered toast and 31 West Hill.[5]

Did the young Betjeman, one wonders, notice the tall – and to a child, elderly – priest, dressed always in a cassock, who likewise gained the 'leafy slope' of West Hill as he returned

98

from his continued visits to the reading room of the British
Museum?

The peace and pleasant surroundings of Highgate village
are sufficient in themselves to explain Woodward's choice in
settling there, but an additional attraction must have been
provided by the proximity of St Augustine's church. Begun in
1887 to the design of the distinguished Anglo-catholic architect John Dando Sedding (1838–1891) – whose brother
Edmund had coincidentally been a priest and a collector of
carols before his early death – St Augustine's like St
Barnabas' Pimlico had been built for ritualistic worship. And
indeed it had a link with St Barnabas' insofar as its Vicar at
this time, the Revd C. G. T. Maturin, had been an assistant
curate there from 1869 to 1880, overlapping with Woodward who went to his curacy at St Barnabas' in 1874. Then
besides finding a familiar kind of worship and an old
colleague at St Augustine's, Woodward would also have been
attracted by the strong musical tradition which had become
established there; just two years earlier the church had
gained a fine three manual organ. It seems that he settled
happily at this church, continuing to assist there for the
remainder of his life.

Only four of Woodward's sermons survive, and so it is
from these alone that his approach and style as a preacher
must be gauged. One of these sermons, preached at St
Barnabas' Pimlico on July 15th 1900, was subsequently
printed, whilst the others – two of which are dated respectively 1916 and 1917, and so come from this period of his
life – survive in manuscript. The fourth, so far as can be
judged by the handwriting and by the absence of a certain
vigour of thought and expression which characterise the
other sermons, probably dates from the last years of his life.[6]
The manuscript sermons are written out in full, which was
probably his custom, and they are not unduly long. They
might be classified as biblical insofar as there is frequent
reference to Holy Scripture; they also contain references
which reflect the preacher's wide reading within the fields of
classical literature, the writings of the Fathers, and English
literature. But the fact that these references are made must
not give the impression that Woodward's preaching was at

all rarified or academic. Indeed the most obvious characteristic of it after its solid biblical foundation is its directness
and practicality. The 1900 sermon provides a good example
of this. The text was Matthew 25.40, and having reminded
his hearers of Jesus' words about feeding the hungry,
giving drink to the thirsty, taking in the stranger, etc., he
continues:

> Six different ways are specified in which this love to Christ
> was shown. They probably include all the possible ways in
> which a man can show love for his fellow-man. And yet there
> are numbers of professed disciples of Our Lord who have no
> idea of charity. Give clothes to a beggar? Not they. Let him go
> to the parish. Give meat to a hungry man? Not they. What do
> we pay rates and taxes for? The idea of giving anything to
> another, or doing anything for another, without getting paid
> for it, or praised for it, seems to be out of all character.
>
> Now selfishness is as much opposed to the spirit of the
> Gospel as the cold of Siberia is to the warmth of the Italian
> sun. If the sun of Christ's love has shone in your hearts, you
> will love others, and will show your love practically by doing
> them good in all sorts of ways – and you do it, for the love of
> Christ constraineth you ...[7]

The admirable directness here is rather different from the
almost harsh language which is found in the 1916 sermon,
preached on July 23rd at St Barnabas' Beckenham. In those
early years of the First World War there had been a move in
certain quarters to encourage, and even to seek to impose,
teetotalism. Woodward took a strong exception to this, and
in this particular sermon he preached with equal vigour
against both drunkenness and enforced total-abstinence. The
sermon began:

> As sermons on Temperance or Teetotalism are being preached
> in many pulpits in our land, and because much intemperate
> language will be used on this subject of temperance, and
> because many well meaning but misguided and ignorant
> persons will be uttering many hard sayings and sentences and
> even blasphemous speeches against one of God's good gifts
> towards mankind, I mean wine, and as much confusion will be
> made, as the handbills bear witness that have been so freely
> distributed here and elsewhere, between drink which is a
> blessing of God, and drunkenness which is a curse of the devil,
> it seems desirable to see and hear what the Church and the

Bible, what the early fathers of the Eastern and Western Church have to say on this subject, irrespective of the teaching of modern heretics and schismatics.

St Paul, Isaiah, Noah, St John Chrysostom, St Augustine of Hippo, and even Fr Benson SSJE, are all quoted from or alluded to, and strong words are used of both the extremes he seeks to combat. As regards the proponents of teetotalism, he declares that 'their arguments are astoundingly weak – weak as water – they say so many millions are spent yearly on alcohol in one form or another: Why not? We might retort, and so many more millions are spent each year on tea, coffee, cocoa and tobacco'. One passage makes direct reference to the War:

> They say that even a little stimulant is bad for the troops in war-time especially. Well brave as the British soldier undoubt- edly is, I doubt if the Russian Cossack who takes of the wine of his country – Vodka excepted, which is really more like a drug than honest wine – or the French soldier who enjoys his Burgundy or Claret, or the Italian who likes his Chianti and cannot work and fight without it, is at all inferior to our own gallant troops.

James Horsfall recalled being told that this sermon had caused 'quite a stir'; apparently Woodward had been asked to preach on abstinence, and took his hearers by surprise in choosing to defend the moderate use of alchohol.

The other surviving sermons, the one of them preached at St Paul's Knightsbridge on January 17th 1917 and the other at St George's Hanover Square, but undated, were both delivered on the occasion of a wedding. In both of them the traditional Christian teaching on marriage is expounded, and the couples are urged to imitate the marriage of Tobit and Sarah, and of other edifying couples in the Old Testament; in the 1917 sermon this pointing to good examples is extended to cover marriages both in classical literature and in the works of Shakespeare. Again in both sermons he urges that the couples should regularly remind themselves of the vows which they have made to each other, saying in 1917 'You will of course read this marriage service over together every year to come' (he crossed out 'for many a year' and had substituted 'every year') 'on this great anniversary of your lives, and ask yourselves, on bended knee, how you are keeping your vows and promises here made in the presence of God, the Holy Angels, and an innumerable company of unseen but true witnesses'. This suggestion of a kind of 'annual review' is a practical suggestion, and its serves to point to an overall picture of Woodward as a practical and essentially 'down to earth' preacher, and one whose primary aim was to apply the traditional teaching of the Bible and the Church to everyday situations.

On the face of it, Woodward seems to have been little affected by the 1914–1918 War; there is no 'war poetry' written by him, no patriotic hymns, and indeed in his printed works the only references to the war are an apology for the late appearance of one book and the curtailment of another, due to wartime conditions. We do not, of course, know the content of his wartime sermons, other than the sermon against drunkenness and total abstinence and the 1917 wedding sermon, the latter of which could hardly be expected to deal with any wartime theme. But given his sensitivity, his interest and loyalty towards his old school and college – so many of whose recent alumni must have been in the casuality lists – and added to this his enthusiasm for the German culture and language, and his preference for the old order, which was manifestly passing away as the war progressed – taken together these things make it seem likely that the Great War affected him deeply. An indication of this may perhaps be seen in the fact that he published no secular verse during the war, nor indeed for some time after it, and that despite his being such a prolific writer, nothing at all appeared from his pen in the years 1915, 1916, or 1918.

Woodward's main occupation during the war years appears to have been the translation of hymns from the Greek Church, and the first fruits of this work was the publication of *The Acathist Hymn of the Holy Orthodox Church in the Original Greek Text and done into English Verse*, which he had undertaken jointly with W. J. Birkbeck. Published by Longmans in 1917 it was bound in paper, had sixty-two pages, and was sold at three shillings and sixpence. Sadly Birkbeck, of whom Lord Halifax wrote 'there was one fact which more than any other distinguished him from his contemporaries. It was his unrivalled knowledge of the East and the Orthodox Church',[8] was dead by the time the book appeared; he had died shortly after his return from a visit to Russia in 1916. Birkbeck was to have written the Preface to the book, which in the event was written by Woodward. In it he explained that Birkbeck had been the instigator of the work: that 'about four years ago the late Mr W. J. Birkbeck chose from Greek and Russian Service Books, a number of hymns and anthems' for translation.

This would have been at about the time when Woodward's translation of St John of Damascus' *Canon for the Repose of the Mother of God* was published, and it may have been this that prompted Birkbeck to encourage Woodward in his 'Englishing', as they both called it, of Orthodox liturgical material. Woodward further explains in the preface that Birkbeck's interests were not solely academic: first, the availability of this material in translation would hopefully encourage a growing-together of Anglicans and Orthodox by familiarising the former with the custom of invoking the Blessed Virgin in prayer, and so help to remove the scandal which their failure to use such prayer presented for the Orthodox. Second, Birkbeck had hoped that a knowledge of the theology enshrined in the material would prove to be a safeguard to sound teaching on the Incarnation, and 'a wholesome corrective to ideas largely borrowed from sixteenth-century Germans such as Luther and Bucer, and from other continental Protestants, like Zwingli and Calvin'.[9] This two-fold purpose, the encouragement of understanding between Orthodoxy and Anglicanism and the safeguarding of orthodox belief in the latter could hardly have failed to appeal to Woodward, whose own practical approach, seen in regard to hymnody in the Prefaces to both *Songs of Syon* and *Piae Cantiones*, is evident here in his statement that he has adopted 'easy metres' in the translation to enable the 'Acathist Hymn' to be sung, adding that 'the writer will gladly help anyone who wishes to sing the hymn'.[10] With the apparent wish to commend the famous seventh-century hymn to an Anglican audience, Woodward provides as footnotes a large number of biblical references

for the images and phrases used in the course of the hymn.
The following is given as a sample of his translation:

> Hail Mary! Star that shall display
> The Sun of Justice' brighter ray:

> Hail Mary! of whose generous womb
> The Word of God doth flesh assume.

> Hail Mary! for, by thee subdued
> The whole creation is renew'd:

> Hail Mary! for the Holy One
> The world's Creator, is thy Son.

> Hail Maid Mother
> Like none other.[11]

In a note at the end of his translation of the *Canon for the
Repose of the Mother of God*, published in 1913, Woodward
had spoken of John Mason Neale as being 'one of the earliest
and most accomplished of the translators of the sacred verse
of the Orthodox communion', and he threw light on Neale's
particular influence upon him when writing the Preface to his
next work after the 'Acathist Hymn', his book *The Most
Holy Mother of God in the Songs of the Eastern Church*,
which was published in 1919. He wrote there in a revealing
passage:

> For more than half a century now I have been an enthusiastic
> lover and admirer of John Mason Neale's hymns of the
> Eastern Church. Acting on his wishes that others should
> follow in his footsteps and translate yet more and more of
> Greek sacred verse, I began twenty years ago to render into
> English certain '*Troparia*' and '*Theotokia*', and some of these
> versions have appeared from time to time in divers periodicals,
> anthologies, and kalendars. But, seeing that, though Neale had
> translated many '*Theotokia*' into prose in his History of the
> Orthodox Eastern Church, he had, with one exception, never
> put into verse any of these songs in honour of the Mother of
> God; and being aware that Neale's successors had for the most
> avoided them altogether (or, worse still, had modified or
> 'Calvinised' them), I thought it high time to turn my attention
> to this particular branch of ecclesiastical poetry.[12]

It is significant that he claims to have known Neale's hymns
for 'half a century', in other words since his time as an undergraduate in Cambridge, and also that he had been making

translations of Greek hymns since the beginning of the
century. Here too is clear evidence that he did indeed see
himself as continuing Neale's work, whilst elsewhere in the
Preface he also presents himself as being concerned to defend
orthodox Christian belief in making these hymns available,
insofar as they so clearly present the truth of the Incarnation,
'a doctrine to be firmly held and vigorously taught in these
days when old heresies are being revived under new forms'.[13]
Finally, having noted that Neale translated hymns concerning the Blessed Virgin into prose, he says – and here we
see him again as no blind follower of his 'master' – why he
believes that verse is preferable to prose: 'Rightly or wrongly,
I believe that, whether the originals be secular epigrams or
sacred poetry, the most literal of renderings into prose are
less attractive to the ordinary readers than translation into
English metrical verse in rhyme – moreover, in this latter
form they lend themselves better to music'.[14] In view of the
very considerable volume of translation into English verse
which Woodward produced over the years, his thinking
expressed in this passage seems to be significant for the
understanding of his purpose.

The volume *The Most Holy Mother of God in the Songs of
the Eastern Church* contains one-hundred and thirty-six
'songs', which had once again been chosen by Birkbeck, who
had then asked Woodward to translate them, something to
which he had 'agreed gladly'. It was, in fact, just part of the
total project to which the translation of the 'Acathist Hymn'
had belonged. Not all of the translations here are happy; one
which exhibits his tendency to use somewhat mannered
archaisms together with rather forced and banal rhymes, is a
song for the Annunciation which concludes with these words
spoken by Blessed Virgin to the Archangel:

> 'Jape me not with word unjust,
> Me, a stranger unto lust,
> Say, by wedlock undefiled,
> How shall Mary bear a child.'[15]

But some of the translations are, it is only fair to say, more
successful artistically, having that same simplicity – even
naivety – which Woodward himself claimed to find so

attractive in ancient carols. The following is perhaps a good
example:

> Today the Virgin cometh
>    In wondrous wise, unheard,
> To child within a cavern,
>    The pre-eternal Word.
>
> Give ear, glad earth! With angels
>    And herds, rejoice, O man!
> Lo! God, a new-born Infant,
>    That was ere time began.[16]

The year 1919 also saw the publication of *The Cowley
Carol Book, Second Series*, in which a number of the additional carols had words which were translations from the
Greek, and in the same year the Faith Press, which had
published *The Most Holy Mother of God*, also published
*Saint George Meglomartyr. In Twenty Hymns of the Holy
and Orthodox Eastern Church, Now First done into English
Verse*. Being only fifteen pages long this was a pamphlet
rather than a book, although the attractive cover, which
shows a woodcut of St George slaying the dragon printed in
red and black, served to give it a certain distinction. There
was considerable interest in Eastern Orthodoxy amongst
Anglo-catholics at the time, and this was one of a series of
pamphlets, other authors included Woodward's friends Athelstan Riley and Walter Frere.[17] As a devout Anglo-catholic,
Woodward's veneration for the saints was unexceptional,
and it is not surprising that he should have had a particular
devotion to his own patron, St George, whom – in his translation – he addressed in the following terms on his feast-day:

> Noblest of noble Martyrs,
>    George, winner of the prize
> Today, in full assembly
>    Thy name we eulogize.
>
> For thou thy course hast ended,
>    And kept the Faith aright,
> And hast of God receivèd
>    Thy Crown of victory bright.
>
> Him pray, from death and danger
>    That safe may be their lot,
> Who celebrate thy Festa,
>    Day ne'er to be forgot.[18]

However such verses may be viewed today, those in *Saint George Meglomartyr* were certainly well-received at St Barnabas' Pimlico, and the note which the Vicar, Hanbury-Tracy, placed in the September 1919 number of the parish magazine is interesting in reflecting both the taste of the time and the affection in which Woodward continued to be held in Pimlico. He wrote 'although it is over twenty years since the Revd G. R. Woodward left St Barnabas' he has still many friends in the parish and congregation who will be glad to hear of some new publications of his which have lately appeared'. Then after giving details of where *St George Meglomartyr* could be obtained, he continued 'Mr Woodward is more than a skilled translator; his work has a touch of genius and while most translations are bald and unattractive those of Mr Woodward read always like original poetry. His studies in Latin and Greek have given his own verse something of the clear-cut perfection of those two languages. The translation of The Acathist Hymn of the Holy Orthodox Eastern Church, which he published two years ago is a masterpiece. Those who do not know it should make the acquaintance of this wonderful tribute of the Eastern Church to our Lady.'

The last item in this group of verse-translations from Orthodox liturgical sources came in 1922; bound in paper, forty pages long, and published by SPCK at the price of two shillings, it was called simply *Hymns of the Greek Church*. There were seventy-three of them, with the Greek and English texts set out side by side, the writer of the introductory note stating that they had already appeared in the journal *The Christian East* between October 1921 and July 1922. He also wrote that Woodward had made the translations at odd times during the past seventeen years, which, roughly fitting in with the claim made by Woodward himself in his Preface to *The Most Holy Mother of God*, further confirms that his interest in Greek hymnody went back to the early years of the century. Again the aim was to make Orthodox writings more familiar, and thereby to confirm the reader in right doctrine – 'It is hoped that (like Neale's *Hymns of the Eastern Church*) this little blue book will give the English reader some fresh ideas as to the vastness and

riches of the Eastern Church's treasury of sacred song, and
will supply people with some few further samples of
Orthodox hymnody and of orthodox theology also'.[19]
Woodward's personal hope, as ever, was that his hymn-translations would be sung , and beneath each item he suggests
where a suitable tune can be found in either *Songs of Syon* or
*The Cowley Carol Book*, something which he had also done
in *St George Meglomartyr*. The collection includes the translation of a further hymn in honour of St George, and this
arguably more successful than the one quoted above:

> Liberator of the slave,
> Leech in time of sickness grave,
> Poor and needy people's shield,
> Friend of kings on battlefield.
>
> Mighty-Martyr, palm in hand,
> Good Saint George, in glory-land
> Plead with Christ, that he may shrive,
> See, and save our souls alive.[20]

It may have been a copy of this last series of translations
from Greek liturgical texts, *Hymns of the Greek Church*,
which Woodward sent to Archbishop Chrysostom of Athens.
He received an acknowledgement, written on January 19th
1926, in which the archbishop wrote 'Your praiseworthy
work will undoubtedly provoke the interest of the pious
English people. It will introduce him [sic] to the glorious
service-books of the Orthodox Eastern Church.'[21]

Woodward had edited the second series of *The Cowley
Carol Book* jointly with Charles Wood, and within five years
of its publication they had collaborated on two further
collections of carols, both of which in the opinion of some
church musicians deserve to be better known. First, in 1920,
came *An Italian Carol Book*, 'being a selection of *Laude
Spirituali* of the XVIth and XVIIth centuries'. The book
contained thirty-seven items, all but four of them
harmonised by Wood himself. The carols were mostly of
what Ian Copley in his book *The Music of Charles Wood* has
called 'the synthetic sort', that is with traditional melodies
accompanied by new words composed for them by
Woodward. Copley is critical of these, writing 'G. R.
Woodward was responsible for the words, and herein lies the

rub. His penchant for the pseudo-archaic is so pronounced as to be, in certain instances, positively ludicrous', and he cites a particularly unfortunate couplet 'Pontius Pilate, ere the break of day, Sat on his doomstool (Weyla wayaway)'. In Copley's opinion, 'if the *Italian Carol Book* could be reissued with new words it might be enormously popular',[22] but in fairness to Woodward, the couplet quoted is hardly typical of his work. Nevertheless, in the letter which Woodward wrote to Wood's widow in December 1926, there is just a suggestion that Wood himself may sometimes have had misgivings about his friend's words: he wrote with reference to the mediaeval carol '*Angelus ad Virginem*', 'Your husband and I talked it over, and he thought it better to give the Latin words only: but I had rendered it, very closely, into the English tongue …' Did Wood perhaps feel on this one occasion at least that it would be better to avoid a Woodward translation? Charles Wood's son Edward remembered his father and Woodward at the time of their collaboration on *An Italian Carol Book*, and his reminiscence provides an example of Woodward's scholarly liking for correctness of language: Edward Wood wrote in a letter 'another day I remember clearly was when I was going home with my father. It must have been in the summer of 1919 when their work on *An Italian Carol Book* was practically finished and ready to go forward to the publisher (Faith Press). My father and I were facing each other in seats next to the window in the 6.15 pm train for Cambridge. The window was lowered so that we could exchange words with the G. R. W., who was seeing us off before catching his train. His final words, as he leant in through the window were to emphasise that the title of the book must be *An Italian Carol Book*, stressing the indefinite article (that title has not always been correctly quoted).'[23]

Four years later, in 1924, Woodward and Charles Wood published *The Cambridge Carol Book. Being Fifty-two Songs for Christmas, Easter, and Other Seasons.* It was the last collection of tunes and verses which Woodward would be involved with, and it was here that his most popular carol 'Ding Dong! Merrily on High' made its first public appearance. The claim on the title page that Woodward and Wood were 'editors' is possibly misleading, since the book was very much their own work. Of the fifty-three items it contains (there is a curious discrepancy between the title and the actual number of items) no less than half the harmonisations are by Wood, with one new tune by him, and with an additional ten harmonisations contributed by Woodward. As regards the words, here no less than thirty of the carols have words newly written by Woodward, with a further thirteen translations – five of the latter being from the Greek. There are only three carols with words by Neale, and one of these has, as Woodward notes, been 'reverently altered here and there to suit an ancient ecclesiastical pre-Reformation melody'. Why, it may be asked, had the proportion of Woodward's own literary compositions grown so markedly since his first carol collections thirty years earlier? If, as regards the ancient Latin carols, he was tending to run out of suitable subjects for translation, that could hardly be said of the Greek religious songs; it seems more likely that by this time he had overcome the diffidence that he claimed to feel at an earlier period, and that he quite simply enjoyed writing verses to be sung as carols.

Besides containing Woodward's best-known carol, *The Cambridge Carol Book* also contains what is perhaps one of his worst – although arguably it is not entirely fair to criticise the words of any carol in isolation from the tune which accompanies it. The carol in question reads:

> From Galilee they came,
> Saint Joseph and his Dame:
> O'er hill they speed, nor dally up valley, up valley:
> O'er hill they speed, nor dally up valley, O la!
>
> When night fell dark and chill,
> And wind 'gan whistle shrill,
> Went Joseph and his Dearie, aweary, aweary,
> Went Joseph and his Dearie, aweary, O la!
>
> Arriv'd in Bethleham,
> There was but found for them
> (The best that they were able) a stable, a stable,
> ('Twas all that they were able) a stable, O la![24]

Of words such as these Mervyn Horder asks, 'Was the true trouble that he was a solitary man with no trusted friend to laugh him out of his excesses?'[25] Perhaps Charles Wood was

too kind and too serious a person to fulfil that role, but
happily lines such as these are far from typical of the general
standard of composition in the collection, and whilst 'From
Galilee they Came' is unlikely to be heard these days, such
carols as 'Past Three A Clock' and 'When an Angel Host
Entuned' continue to be used and to find acceptance. One
composition which has, like certain of Neale's carols, a
decidedly 'gothic-revival' feeling about it certainly deserves
to be better known:

> Outside, how hard it bloweth,
>   The nor' nor' eastern gale!
> Outside, how fast it snoweth!
>   'Twill freeze the milk in pail.
> Ay me! how dark the night!
>   Nay, e'en when day do lengthen,
>   (Men say) the cold will strengthen,
> Ere summer draw in sight.
>
> Indoors, meanwhile, 'tis merry,
>   Men trim the house with spray
> Of rud red holly berry,
>   Or green-leaf of the bay.
> To curb the winter cold,
>   The spit is set a-turning;
>   The yule block too is burning,
> As in the days of old.
>
> In hall, despite the weather,
>   Goodwill and warmth abound:
> There hearts are knit together
>   With Carol, Glee and Round,
> In worship of that morn,
>   When God was (in December,
>   As grateful folk remember)
> Of Maiden Mary born.[26]

Woodward was seventy-six years old when *The
Cambridge Carol Book* was published, and together with
two other books which appeared in 1924 it would be his last
commercial publication. After that year he produced a
considerable number of booklets, but these were all privately
printed and were probably never on public sale. One of those
two other books from 1924 was *Acta Sanctorum*, which was
published by Mowbrays and consisted of twelve poems, of
varying length. In the same way that the words in *The*

*Cambridge Carol Book* were predominently his own compositions rather than translations – as they had been in earlier
collections of carols – so too in *Acta Sanctorum*. It seems
almost to be a sequel to his 1898 volume *Legends of the
Saints*; the sometimes fairly lengthy narrative poems, written
in rhyming couplets, being of the same form and having the
same kind of subject. But again despite the title he does not
confine himself strictly to legends of the Saints, and whilst
there are stories of St Barbara, St Swithun and St John
Chrysostom, Noah and Abraham also appear as subjects,
together with a verse account of the Marriage at Cana and
the legend of the Crown Imperial. His interest in bees
continues, one of the pieces having the title 'Babe Ambrose
and the Swarm of Bees'. Some lines from this may serve to
give a flavour of the book:

> Befel it so, upon a day
> Babe Ambrose in his cradle lay;
> Where, for to stint him of his weep,
> His mother rockt her child to sleep.
> While there he slept with open mouth,
> Lo! were it from the north or south,
> Borne on the balmy summer-breeze,
> There came a swarm of golden bees.
> Well seen by many in that place,
> They settled harmless on his face,
> and throng'd within and out full blive.
> As though his mouth had been their hive,
> But after soon they took to flight
> Aloft, and vanish's out o sight.
>    Hereon old Ambrose in delight
> Made prophecy, with reason right:
> 'This silly babe one day', said he,
> 'A marvellous worthy man shall be'.[27]

Phrases such as 'to stint him of his weep' showed that
Woodward had lost none of his liking for the quaint and
curious form of words, whilst the subject of the piece seems
to indicate that ingenuousness which was an attractive
feature of his personality. The opening of two of the other
poems might suggest that they were written with children in
mind, 'San Giovanni Gualberto or the Forgiving Knight' for
example begins with the words:

> Now, Christian children, sit ye still,
> And hearken if it be your will,
> And ye shall hear a tale of mine
> About a certain Florentine ... [28]

However, this is more likely to be a literary conceit rather than a serious attempt to write for children again as he did in *Cock Robin and Jenny Wren*.

*Acta Sanctorum* was very much a continuation of the kind of work which Woodward had done before, but a third of those three final books which appeared in 1924 was something rather different. It was called *The Adoration of The Kings depicted by The Great Masters*, and it consisted of a series of plates accompanied by some twenty-seven 'carols', which, since Woodward appeared on the title-age as editor, must presumably have been chosen by him. In reality they would be better described as Christmas Poems rather than carols, including as they do such items as Robert Southwell's 'The Burning Babe' and Sir Walter Scott's 'Christmas in the Olden Time'. Woodward limited himself to just one contribution; entitled 'A Christmas Carol', but it, like the other pieces in the book is hardly a carol in any accepted sense. It begins:

> On Twelfth-Day morn, old Christmas-Day,
> Ere mid-night scarce be past away,
> 'Tis by our country folk averr'd,
> And let no scoffer doubt their word,
> That, oft as Yule-time wheeleth round,
> The bees in hive, by weather bound,
> Hum, only on this night, for mirth,
> In worship of our Saviour's birth:
> That, as aforetime, even now
> Both ox & ass before him bow: –
> That, in remembrance of that dawn,
> When unto herdmen on the lawn
> Good news was by an Angel told,
> The sheep, confined within the fold,
> Face east-ward, while their kin without
> Gang in procession round about: –
> That on this night the forster sees
> The deer a-falling on their knees: – ...[29]

Somewhat oddly, after having continued in the same vein, the poem ends rather abruptly, as if curtailed or unfinished. The

book was published by the art-printing firm The Medici
Society, which had been brought into being by Philip Lee
Warner, a relative of Woodward's wife, but it is chiefly of
interest insofar as it provides some kind of indication as to
Woodward's own taste in poetry. He clearly favoured
Southwell, three of whose poems are chosen, and also Robert
Herrick, who has the same number of pieces in the collection
and who Woodward quoted in one of the surviving sermons.
Indeed the major part of the poetry here comes from English
writers of the late sixteenth and early seventeenth centuries,
and includes work by Shakespeare, Wither, Milton, Jonson,
and Drummond. It would be interesting to know whose idea
this illustrated anthology was: if Woodward's, then it might
have its origin in Birkbeck's original intention for *The
Acathist Hymn*, which, according to its Preface, was to have
been illustrated by pictures of 'Russian Eikons which Mr W.
J. Birkbeck brought back from Petrograd in 1916 for this
edition', but which intention was frustrated by wartime
economies. That Woodward had some interest in religious
art is also suggested by the fact that in his will he left the
National Gallery 'the small Oil Painting of the Holy Family
now in my drawing room said to be of the Bolognese or
Roman School'.[30]

Two years before the publication of *The Cambridge Carol
Book, Acta Sanctorum*, and *The Adoration of The Kings*,
Woodward made an acquisition which would occupy his
time and interest until the end of the decade. This was a small
printing press, which James Horsfall remembered as being
installed in one of the bedrooms at 48 West Hill. Woodward
used it to print a whole series of small booklets, and these
became an outlet for his new compositions and translations.
All of these booklets were bound in thick paper, usually of a
buff colour, but occasionally dark brown, rust, or green;
under his name on the title page of the first to appear he
proudly placed the words 'printed by the above at 48 West
Hill, Highgate Village'. The series began with a group of
three booklets containing words for carols: *Carols for Yule-
tide* in 1922, and in the following year *The Babe of
Bethlehem, Being some Christmas Carols*, followed by *The
Mother of My Lord, or Carols for Our Lady*. Over the years

he produced at least thirty-five of these booklets, but only one other, his *Good Friday and Easter-day Couplets*, 1924, came up to the same artistic standard of the initial three. These are beautifully set out, printed, and decorated with woodcuts, in very much the way that his first collection of *Carols for Christmas-tide* had been in 1892. That collection had been printed by Pickering & Chatto, and it is tempting to speculate as to whether the Mr. A. Oliver who he acknowledges as having helped him with *Carols for Yule-tide* and *The Babe of Bethlehem* had been connected with that firm. As indeed it is tempting to wonder whether in this printing venture Woodward might possibly have been influenced by the memory of G. H. Palmer's father, the friend of J. M. Neale, who many years before had been a printer in Cambridge.

Some very brief 'Explanatory Notes' at the beginning of *Carols for Yule-tide* announce that the edition is limited to one hundred and eight copies; they also tell the reader that 'In every instance, the Words of the Carol have been written with an eye to some old-fashioned Tune, and Setting, which, if ever published, will be found melodious'. In the event *Carols for Yule-tide* proved to be a preparatory for *The Cambridge Carol Book* published two years later, since no less than nine out of the fourteen sets of words found a place there; similarly six out of the twenty items in *The Babe of Bethlehem* were incorporated into *The Cambridge Carol Book*, but only two from *The Mother of My Lord*. Both of these two, however, continue in use – 'There stood in Heaven a Linden Tree' and 'When an Angel Host Entuned', as of course have 'Ding Dong! Merrily on High' and 'Past Three A Clock', which were first printed in *Carols for Yule-tide*. *The Babe of Bethlehem* was also given 'Explanatory Notes', in which Woodward wrote 'As in *Carols for Yule-tide*, the peculiar measures, rhythms, & rimes of some of these Carols are to be accounted for by the Editor's continued & honest endeavour to preserve the integrity of the ancient melodies to which alone, respectively, they should be sung'. Since, however, no tunes were specified when the booklet was produced, this last would have been rather difficult to comply with, although in view of the fact that just two-hundred numbered copies were printed, and these were presumably not placed on sale, the problem remains academic. It is interesting that *The Babe of Bethlehem*, unlike the two other booklets, was given a dedication: 'To the memory of his Father George Ratcliffe Woodward and of his Mother Anne Deville Woodward'. Sadly, one or two of the verses which seem to have real merit, have remained largely unknown. One such is this:

> A Galley will I build me,
>   A brave ship, and a fine:
> With rudder, oar, and main-sail,
>   And cross-tree mast, of pine.
>
> Now who shall be my skipper?
>   Jesus, my lover kind;
> Will save my barque from ship-wreck,
>   According to his mind.
>
> Our Lady she must steer it,
>   Saint Mary, Virgin-queen,
> Fraught with her heavenly burthen,
>   The Pearl of price, I mean.
>
> And whom to choose for pilot?
>   My guiding Angel-star
> Shall see his convoy safely
>   In port across the bar.
>
> So shall my gallant Galley
>   Arrive at that fair coast,
> Where reigneth God, the Father,
>   The Son, the Holy Ghost.[31]

Finding himself free from the strictures of a commercial publisher, Woodward lapsed into his old ways of using the 'Long-S' in these three booklets, something which was, of course, corrected in the case of those carols which found their way into *The Cambridge Carol Book*. For him, the term 'old-fashioned' bore no suggestion of criticism, rather the reverse.

Four more booklets appeared in 1924. Of these, *Good Friday and Easter-day Couplets*, which has already been mentioned, is both very small and finely set-out and printed. As the title suggests, it falls into two sections, each containing couplets which recall Old Testament types of the

Cross and of the Resurrection respectively. Also small, but without the woodcuts which decorate the three carol collections and the couplets, is a translation from the writings of the fourth-century Greek father St Gregory of Nazianzus. It is entitled *Low Sunday at Gangra of Paphlagonia*, and perhaps Woodward was moved to translate it because of the four verses which speak of bees: two of these read ...

> Now doth the busy bee full blive
> Unlock her wing, and quit her hive
>    For meadow green and sunny;
> Displaying marv'lous-worthy wit,
> While hither, thither, she doth flit,
>    Despoiling flowers of honey.

> In season she will never cease
> To labour hard, and make increase
>    Of nectar-syrup ample;
> And O that man in Jesu's hive
> Might at such industry arrive,
>    And follow bee's example![32]

A third and rather larger booklet which Woodward printed in 1924 – its pages number to ninety-one – is entitled *133 Love-epigrams in English Verse from the Greek Antholgy*. This is the first of a whole series of translations into verse made from the Greek classical writings, several coming from the Anthology, and on the title-page he appropriately describes himself as 'Formerly Scholar of Gonville & Caius College Cambridge'. Epigrams seem to have fascinated him; as early as 1903 his book *Poemata* had contained a poem entitled 'Suggested by a Greek Epigram'.

The year 1924 not only saw the result of Woodward and Wood's final collaboration in the publication of *The Cambridge Carol Book*, but also the achievement of a particular distinction by both men within the field of music. In that year, Charles Wood finally succeeded to the chair of Music in the University of Cambridge, whilst Woodward was awarded the Lambeth degree of Doctor of Music. By a privilege which dates back to the sixteenth-century, and which stems from the Archbishopric of Canterbury having abrogated to itself certain rights which were formerly exercised by the papacy in England, the holder of the highest office in the Church of England is entitled to bestow degrees *in honoris causa*. These, known as Lambeth degrees, have continued to be awarded sparingly, and only in recognition of real distinction. The suggestion that Woodward should be honoured in this way came from the well-known Organist of the Temple Church, Sir Henry Walford Davies, who at the end of 1923 wrote a letter to the then-Archbishop, Randall Davidson, in which he said:

> Pardon me if I suggest that there is a man to whom the Honorary Degree of Doctor of Music could so fittingly be given that I should be most grateful if I might be allowed to do anything that is necessary to make it easy for your Grace to bestow it. I refer to the Revd G. R. Woodward the editor of a wonderful collection of Tunes called *Songs of Syon*. I think he must be over seventy. He is an erudite, devout musical scholar.
>
> He has no idea that anyone has approached your Grace, nor has any friend suggested that I write. I feel sure Sir Walter, Hugh Allen and others would heartily agree. May I do anything further to help in this matter?[33]

Archbishop Davidson replied to this letter on January 2nd 1924, recalling that 'Woodward was at Harrow with me and was a companion in the Sixth Form for a couple of years'. Besides Walford Davies the two other people who formally supported the plea were the Bishop of Ripon, the Rt Revd T. B. Strong, and Sir William Hadow, a musician who was at that time Vice-Chancellor of the University of Sheffield; the same three men who – in company with Sir Edward Elgar and the Poet Laureate Robert Bridges – had made a similar and successful plea for the doctorate of music to be conferred upon Woodward's old friend G. H. Palmer in 1917. Hadow's submission to the Archbishop is interesting and worthy of quotation because it testifies both to Woodward's abilities and to the high regard in which he was held at the time in the world of English church music, a regard which is easily forgotten with the passing of the years. In his letter to the Archbishop, Hadow wrote:

> I cannot think of anyone in England on whom such a Degree could better be bestowed. Mr Woodward has for many years done admirable work in the field of Church Music. His *Songs of Syon* and his *Cowley Carol Book* are two of the best collections that have ever been edited. He has brought to the work

not only wide knowledge and sound and scholarly discrimina-
tion, but musical and poetic powers of the highest kind.
Through all these years he has worked so quietly and unob-
trusively that he is only now beginning to receive the public
recognition that he deserves. But to all who are concerned in
the study of Church Music and are desirous of maintaining its
level of dignity, purity and reverence, his name has long been
held in high regard.

Following these submissions, Davidson agreed that
Woodward would be a worthy recipient of the degree, and
wrote to him on March 19th with characteristic grace and
*gravitas* to ask whether he would accept such an honour,
beginning his letter by saying 'It is of curious interest to me
to look back across the years to the Harrow Sixth Form, and
to consider how independent of one another our pathways in
life have been. I now write to re-create a link if you will let
me do so ...' The reply which Woodward returned must be
quoted in full, not only because it is one of the comparatively
few letters of his to have survived, but also because it
provides a telling insight into his personality. Writing from
Highgate on March 21st 1924 he replied:

> Your Grace's letter came as a surprise; and I need hardly say
> how grateful I am for it; for your allusion to our Harrow days,
> and for the high honour that you offer me. It was John Farmer
> (whom our beloved & revered Dr Butler brought to Harrow)
> who first taught me to admire Palestrina & Bach & to study
> and love good Church music.
>
> Really I am unworthy of the good opinion that Sir Walford
> Davies, Sir William Hadow, & other eminent musicians seem
> to have of my work: and I was quite content to go on plodding
> away without notice, or such distinction as you are ready to
> give me. But, as it is your Grace's desire, and apparently the
> wish of many of my friends, I have the pleasure to inform you
> that, if you offer me the degree of Doctor of Music, *Honoris
> Causa*, I think that I can see my way to accepting it. For I feel
> that this generous act of yours would not be done to the Revd
> G. R. Woodward but rather it would be, on the part of the
> Church of England, & of her highest authority, a recognition
> of the better sort of Ecclesiastical Music, for which I have for
> many years laboured. If with any small success, I can only
> sing, with William Byrde, *non nobis domine*, etc.
>
> Another reason for my not refusing your offer. I take it that
> your Grace would be paying a compliment to the School on

> the Hill, an old Harrovian honouring another old Harrovian. Also it would be a pleasure to the Master of Gonville & Caius College Cambridge (himself an old Harrow boy, Sayer Scholar, & now also a Governor of the School) to know that a member of his College was receiving the high distinction which your Grace now offers me. Again, many thanks.

Here as elsewhere we see his reticence and self-effacement, his unaffected humility and his devotion to his old school and college, besides something of that sense of mission which he had as regards church music. Davidson wrote the following day to thank him for his 'delightful letter', and the degree was duly conferred at Lambeth on May 12th 1924. The reaction of the Master of Gonville and Caius is unrecorded, but the awarding of the degree certainly gave considerable pleasure at St Barnabas' Pimlico. The May 1924 issue of the parish magazine contained the heading 'Bravo!', under which was printed:

> We find ourselves addressing thus no less a personage than His Grace, the Lord Archbishop of Canterbury! Yes, we Barnabites are impelled to say Bravo, your Grace, because you have bestowed upon one who is dear to us, and of whom we are justly proud, once a faithful Assistant-Priest of S.Barnabas', the dignity of a Mus.Doc. What your predecessor did for the Revd George Palmer, our former Priest-Organist, that you have done for our former Precentor.
>
> We are grateful. The Revd George Ratcliffe Woodward is so well-known in the musical world that no explanation of the honour he has received is required. His numerous publications, amongst which are some rare gems, translations of both Latin and Greek poems, as well as unknown melodies collected from the treasures of the British Museum, his refined taste, his critical ability, have made him what he is to those who find in his writings the reverence of the mediaevalist, the devotion of the mystic, and the touch of the artist.
>
> So we say Bravo, Dr Woodward! You have won what you deserve. May you live long to enjoy your fresh dignity, and serve the Catholic Church of England by continuing to place at her disposal your music, your poetry, and your experience.

It is rather touching, and telling, too, that he should have continued to be remembered at St Barnabas' with such affection a quarter of a century after he had ceased to serve there. And if there is something of naivety in the magazine notice, then there is that, too, in his own reaction to the award: nearly all of his publications in that year and subsequently carried the letters Mus.Doc. after his name, and give the impression that he took a special delight as well as pride in the award which had been made to him. But as 'V.N.G.', the writer of his 'Funeral Tribute' in the *Eastern Daily Press* noted ten years later, whilst he was 'entirely without ambition' he would have been 'more than human if he was not gratified when in 1924 the Archbishop of Canterbury gave him the honorary degree of Doctor of Music'.

The year 1924 seems to mark something of a watershed in Woodward's life. It saw both him and his friend Charles Wood honoured in the world of music, as well as the elevation of his old friend Walter Frere, to the bishopric of Truro. He must, too, have taken pleasure in the three publications of that year, *The Cambridge Carol Book*, *Acta Sanctorum*, and *The Adoration of The Kings*, as well as in the first-fruits of his newly-found hobby of printing. Yet this year also saw the ending of his long and distinguished work with hymns and carols, and ahead, inevitably, lay the loss of friends through death and the gradual weakening of his own physical and intellectual powers. The shadow which must have been cast over this otherwise happy year by the partial destruction of St Augustine's Highgate by fire, with the loss of all its vestments, most of its furnishings, and above all so far as Woodward was concerned, its fine organ, may have seemed to him to be some kind of pressage of the inevitable sadnesses and losses which must lie ahead.

# CHAPTER EIGHT

# THE FINAL YEARS 1925–1934

Woodward's interests may have been somewhat limited, but his attention to them was certainly consistent. An obvious example would be his enthusiasm for plainsong. During the first quarter of the century the Plainsong and Medieval Music Society, of which he had been a founder member in 1888, went through a period of relative inactivity. During that time its Council became what Dom Anselm Hughes has called a 'learned group of "Sarum" scholars', with its attention largely focussed upon the preparation of the fascimile edition of the *Sarum Antiphoner* which was finally published in 1924, and apart from this the Society's only other significant productions were the *Pars Antiphonarii* in 1923 and Woodward's own edition of *Piae Cantiones* in 1910. Membership of the Society had fallen from two-hundred and thirty-nine in 1900 to fifty-six in 1926, and Woodward was one of only five or six council members who regularly attended meetings.[1] In 1926 the Anglican Dom Anselm Hughes, a monk of Pershore, later Nashdom, became Secretary, and something of a revival of the Society's fortunes began to take place. Hughes wished to broaden the base of the Society, not least by involving Catholic as well as Anglican scholars and enthusiasts, and he recalled that Woodward had been 'cordially enthusiastic' in supporting him in this. Walter Frere was Chairman, of whom the distinguished plainsong scholar Dr J. H. Arnold remembered that 'meetings of the Council of the Plainsong Society were always enlivened by his presence – his smile, his sparkle, his humour, his shrewd business sense; but above all, his profound knowledge which sat so lightly on him, and was always at anybody's disposal'.[2] By this time Frere had ceased to practise composition, probably realising – according to his friend Sir Sydney Nicholson – that his musical gifts did not lie in that particular direction.[3] Woodward may have shared this opinion, since the harmonisation which Frere had supplied in 1894 for 'This Joyful Eastertide' in *Carols for*

*Easter and Ascension-tide* was replaced in *The Cowley Carol Book*, seven years later, by a superior harmonisation made by Wood. But whilst Nicholson remembered that Frere did not 'see eye to eye' with G. H. Palmer in later years, there is no suggestion of any disagreement between Frere and Woodward, and Hughes recalled that Woodward remained a 'constant attendant' at meetings of the Council until his resignation in 1932. It seems that by then his activities, including the use of his printing press, were being curtailed through uncertain health, and so his membership of the Council, which stretched back nearly thirty years, came to an end.

The year which saw the rejuvenation of the Plainsong and Mediaeval Music Society, 1926, also saw the death of two of Woodward's oldest and closest friends, G. H. Palmer and Charles Wood. After the first decade of the century Palmer did not attend the council meetings of the Society regularly; he had lived in Oxford since 1917, and was engaged until just before his death, at the age of eighty, on his most significant work *The Diurnal Noted*. He and Woodward may have seen little of each other in the last few years of his life, but it is difficult to imagine that they had not continued to correspond with each other, and that Woodward was not greatly saddened by his friend's death. He had, however, been able to see Wood from time to time. Edward Wood recalled having gone to London with his father on various occasions to attend events at the Royal College of Music, when 'Dr Woodward would accompany us finally to King's Cross, where we would catch our train home to Cambridge and he his local train to Highgate'. Interestingly, Edward Wood continues 'On one such occasion when I happened to be alone with him he warned me wisely of the possibility that some who through envy might not be altogether generously disposed might take advantage of my father's total reluctance to stand up and fight for himself'.[4] Here is seen that shrewdness which is not at all at variance with the genuine unworldliness to which the Christian aspires. Neither of Wood's children remembered Woodward ever visiting their home in Cambridge, but it seems that their father did visit Woodward at Highgate. Again Edward Wood recalled 'My own visit to

Dr Woodward's house was during the year 1927, after my father's death. I was touched then by his description of one of the last visits my father had paid to him there, when, his health failing in his last few years, my father had felt too unwell to do more than lie and rest at length on the sofa. It was obvious how concerned the older man had felt. There was clearly a very strong bond of affection and sympathy as well as of mutual respect and admiration between them. They were indeed devoted friends with a very deeply shared interest in the work in which they collaborated. That they were members of Caius College, Cambridge, albeit not contemporaries, must have strengthened the bond'. Edward Wood summed up his own impression of his father's friend by saying 'My abiding memory of Dr Woodward is of an impressively "good" man, of unshakeable moral principles whose affection and devotion and shared scholarly enthusiasm must have been of greater support to my father than we can ever judge'.

It was Gonville and Caius College which provided one very happy occasion for Woodward in the following year, 1927. He had apparently been invited to the annual Commemoration Feast at the college, and on the previous day the Master had telegraphed him asking him to respond to the toast to the guests. His speech, written out in full like his sermons, has survived.[5] It would seem to have been well-suited to the occasion, containing sincere but not excessive expressions of loyalty, nostalgia, and sentiment; it was of moderate length, and leavened with several humorous allusions. Indeed the content has a graciousness of expression and indeed an urbanity which does credit to the man who composed it – at short notice – when he was almost eighty years old. As might be expected, the speech contains references to his old school and to Dr Butler 'my beloved and revered old master at Harrow'; likewise to Shakespeare, and to the seventeenth-century divine Bishop Jeremy Taylor (one of whose poems had been included in *The Adoration of The Kings*) whom he calls 'a great and shining light'. Charles Wood is named as 'so distinguished an ornament' of the College. But above all it is the institution itself which he praises, and towards which in one paragraph he shows a rather unusual form and degree of loyalty, writing:

> There is one thing that I should like to assure our Hosts, that though we their guests have gone down for good, those ever so many years, yet our love of the college increases ever more and more, striking its roots deeper and deeper into the ground of our hearts and affections. And yet another thing to be remembered. We, your guests, though we are no longer in Cambridge, whenever we are called upon to vote in the Senate House, on some important measure connected with the welfare of the Varsity, to speak for myself, & I think for my fellow guests, we may assure the Master and Fellows that before we cast our votes, this way or that, we make it a point of honour & duty to ascertain first what our Founders and benefactors wishes would be, what the feelings of the best, oldest & wisest of the College Dons & Professors may be; and sometimes pocketing our own private inclinations, we vote accordingly, thereby, I trust, proving ourselves not unworthy of the confidence of the vote which Alma Mater continues to give us, her faithful & obedient children'.

This rather surprising assertion gives a useful insight into the temper of Woodward's mind: there is here a reverence for authority, and a readiness to submit himself to it, which is wholly consonant with the theological convictions which he held as a Catholic Christian. He is seen to have the humility not to make his own opinion the final arbiter when searching for what is right and true.

For the Church of England at large the year 1927 was dominated by the matter of Prayer Book revision. Many had come to feel that the 1662 Book of Common Prayer no longer sufficed to meet the pastoral and liturgical needs of the Church, and after some years of discussion the bishops presented a new book to the Convocations of Canterbury and York on February 7th, only for it to be rejected in the House of Commons on December 15th. The so-called 'Deposited Book' failed to satisfy many of the Evangelicals in the Church of England, who felt that it went too far in a 'Catholic' direction, whilst it was similarly unacceptable to many Anglo-catholics who felt that it did not go far enough, so that not for the last time the conservatives on both flanks of the Church found themselves in an uneasy alliance.

Predictably, Woodward had strong feelings on the matter, which he referred to in his Gonville and Caius speech. This reference occurred through his mention of Bishop John Cosin (1594–1672), a former member of the college, who, he said 'had a big finger in the Prayer Book of 1662, now unhappily under revision, not for the better (so me think) but for the worse'. Woodward was involved personally in one of the outer ripples of the dispute through his membership of the Council of the Plainsong and Mediaeval Music Society. Its chairman, Bishop Frere, was initially an enthusiastic advocate of Prayer Book revision – indeed it was on account of this enthusiasm, coupled with his extensive knowledge of liturgy, that Archbishop Davidson had been so keen that he should join the bench of bishops. Frere had wanted the Society to both prepare and to print music to accompany the new book, holding, apparently, that since the book would most likely come into use whether or not it received authorisation, it would be best to have the correct music ready for issue. The others members of the Council, including Woodward, opposed him on this, being quite willing that the music be prepared, but not that it should be printed prior to the outcome of the debate being known.[6]

Meanwhile Woodward continued to print small booklets containing his verses, these being as ever a mixture of translation and original composition. The number of booklets per year seems to have varied considerably, perhaps according to his state of health. So far as it is possible to tell, whilst there were three each in 1925 and 1926, six in both 1928 and 1931, and a record seven in 1929, none appeared in 1927 or 1930.[7] The majority of the booklets contain verse translations from the Greek classics, with Woodward particularly liking to translate epigrams into verse; six of the seven from 1929 and five of the six from 1931 are translations from the Greek. They have titles such as *Some Remnants of Greek Comedy*, *A Bunch of Grapes from Ancient Greek Vineyards*, and *Greek Witticisms Told in English verse*, all three of which appeared in 1929. It is as if he was continuing to look back nostalgically to his time as a classicist at Harrow and Cambridge, and indeed one of the booklets, *Some Remnants of Greek Comedy*, is dedicated 'In memory of his learned, revered and beloved Masters in classics, while he was their pupil at Harrow-on-the-Hill from A.D.1863–1868', six of whom are then listed. Surprisingly, perhaps, only one of the booklets is wholly given to his earlier interest in Greek Orthodox liturgical material, although the occasional translation from this source is found in his general verse collections. The one booklet is *Sanctorale Parvulum, or Some Greek Church Versicles rimed in English Measures*, printed in 1925, and which he dedicated to the memory of Thomas Helmore, J. R. Lunn, and W. J. Blew, whose harmonisations and translations respectively he had used in his carol collections. It contains brief and rather curious rhymes for feast-days, running through the year from January to December. That for St Timothy, for example, reads:

> Full keen in heaven to be crown'd
> Saint Timothy was beat
> With bloody cudgels, till the ground
> Lay red below his feet.[8]

Whilst well outnumbered by verse translations from the Greek, the half-dozen or so booklets containing other verses are perhaps the more interesting. No less than three of these were printed in 1928: two, entitled *Carmina Spiritualia* and *Translations of Italian, French & German Poems*, are made up of verses from an impressively wide range of sources, but the third, *Miscellaneous Verse Sacred and Secular* consists of his own compositions, some of which are humorous. There is, for example, 'Little Mary at the Apothecary's Shop':

> Of Castor-oil two pen'orth, sir;
> A dear two pen'orth make it:
> An e-wee dose, for I be her
> As is condemn'd to take it.[9]

And there are others in which the eighty-year-old poet recalls with humour places which he had known well in the past. One such is entitled 'To British Museum Male Readers':

> If e're ye be found
> In the Reading-room Round,
>   Remember the bachelor Preedy,
> Whose fore-foot was lamed,
> And his heart-string unframed,
>   By the fall of an Encyclopedy.

'Twas Edna the fair,
With flaxen fine hair,
    Was studying under the dome,
When, out of command,
Dropt out of her hand
    A weighty historical tome.

'So sorry,' said she:
'No matter,' said she:
    But mark, a few days after those,
On her finger a ring,
All along of the thing,
    Let fall, as befel't, on his toes.[10]

But of special interest and attractiveness, and maybe with something of the same feel as some of the verses which would be written by his former neighbour on West Hill, John Betjeman, is a poem which he had composed for one John Russell, 'After Fifty Years in the Quire of Saint Barnabas, Pimlico'. The opening verses read:

Not out, Fifty! Raise your score
Yet an other twenty more!
Faithful Johnnie, good my friend,
Greeting to you here I send.

John Russell, still at even-fall
In smoking-room, or concert-hall,
When work is o'er, the beards wag all,
    You, blithe and bonny,
Bear part in glee or madrigall,
    And pipe HEY NONNY.

Yet not hereof to-day I rime,
But when we twain, in youthful prime,
At Mattins, Mass, or Vesper-chime,
    Whate're the weather,
In Church, in Quire, in olden time.
    Oft sang together.

Here no *base* metal. True your ways
Ring as the *tenor* of your lays:
In fine white linen when you raise,
    And all for love,
In Plain-song note, the hymn of praise
    To Christ above.[11]

These booklets do not contain Prefaces, nor for the most part, notes. There was, however, a brief note placed at the back of two booklets which were printed in 1929, *St Halward the Martyr* and *The Story of Arion and the Dolphin*. The former is an edifying verse-legend of the kind which had appeared in *Legends of the Saints* and in *Acta Sanctorum*; Woodward notes in this case 'Taken from John Mason Neale's *Tales of the Apostles' Creed*. That is in prose; this in verse, but often-times repeating *ipsissima verba magistri*'. Whilst at the back of *The Story of Arion and the Dolphin* he noted 'This little Poem is based on the narratives of Herodotus, Aelian, and Plutarch. But if there is any additional beauty in the duologues and imagery of this old-world fable, as here versified, it is chiefly due to the industry and skill of The Revd John Mason Neale, who has well told the tale of Arion and the Dolphin [written in prose] in his *Stories from Heathen Mythology*. q.v.' A graceful and indeed a final tribute to his 'master'. But what most of the booklets do have at the back of them is a statement of how many copies had been printed, to which the number of the individual copy has been added by pen. *Carmina Spiritualia* for example has printed 'This is to certify you, gentle reader, that only One hundred & Thirty Copies of these *Cantica Spiritualia* have been printed, whereof this particular impression is Number ...' More often the number printed was one hundred and twenty, and the number does not seem to have gone above one-hundred and thirty-six except in the case of *The Babe of Bethlehem*, printed in 1923, of which two hundred copies were made. Perhaps this raises the question of what Woodward had in mind in making these booklets. Essentially they should probably be seen as simply the fruits of an enjoyable hobby which might be shared with friends as the occasion suggested, for there is no reason to suppose that they were ever put on public sale. And yet in a letter of October 16th 1929, in which he mentions 'the hours of pleasant labour' which the production of the booklets had given him, he strikes what is at least a semi-commercial note when he writes: 'It is believed that some of my verse (which I have printed here) will one day be better known, and will fetch a good price, especially as I have printed off only 120

copies or so of each of the 25 booklets.' At the time of his
death there must have been a stock of these booklets at West
Hill, which were later dispersed. The present author has
spoken to two people with a professional interest in books
who have mentioned coming across batches of them in
second-hand bookshops, in one case in North London in
1957. The booklets are now of considerable interest to those
who collect the productions of private presses; they are also
a tribute to Woodward's skill and taste, exercised at an age
when many people would not wish to pursue such a stren-
uous and exacting hobby.

Not, however, that he was unaided in his printing opera-
tions. James Horsfall recalled that once Woodward had set
up the type, the press would be operated by his housekeeper,
Miss Holder. There were in fact two presses in the house,
and in the letter quoted above, written to his executrix,
Woodward directed that 'My largest printing press (Gem
No. 3) goes to Caius Coll. Cambridge, together with all my
type, etc. The Excelsior Press I leave to Holder, who has
helped me greatly with my printing-work & binding, etc.'
Harriet Sarah Holder – called 'Mrs', James Horsfall recalled,
according to the custom of the time 'for decency's sake' – was
described in his will as 'my good and faithful housekeeper'
and he said of her in the above letter 'My faithful & good
servant Holder deserves the best of places as cook, housekeeper, nurse, or travelling companion, in a good family'.
That she worked for Woodward for most if not all of his
eighteen years in Highgate is suggested by a reference to her
in the Gonville and Caius after-dinner speech of 1927.
Having mentioned the college boats, he continued:

> This reminds me of a good and true story. A few years ago
> the Lady Marguerite boat was going well at Henley Regatta
> when one of the crew (a Highgate man and fine oar) had the
> misfortune to catch a crab. I read the paragraph to my cook-
> housekeeper (who happened to know the offending oarsman).
> Quite seriously said she 'Dear me, Sir, what a clever gentleman
> Mr So & So must be to have caught alive a crab, and that too
> in fresh water, while the boat was travelling at such a pace!'

Miss Holder was the only resident staff at 48 West Hill; she
was a Cockney, and James Horsfall recalled that she was

short and dumpy, with a tendency to drop and add 'H's', referring for example to the "igh Halter'. An incessant talker and possessed of a 'heart of gold', it was the custom for her to come into the drawing room for coffee after dinner each evening. Her duties included taking the cairn terrier 'Jamie' for his daily walk, and Woodward told his executrix that after his death Holder 'would like the clock in my bedroom; also Jamie the Cairn'. Presumably he was an attractive animal, because in an undated letter from this period Woodward refers to a lady who gave him lifts to church in her motor-car, adding engagingly 'She and Jamie are sworn friends, & we call her his God-mother'.

James Horsfall's mother and Woodward's executrix, Violet Annie Horsfall, was the daughter of Woodward's half-sister Annie Stewart, afterwards Eaton. Described in his will as 'my dearest and eldest Niece and god-daughter', she lived at Cliff House, Dunwich, on the Suffolk coast, and is still remembered for an incident which occurred in July 1930. According to her son, Violet Horsfall, then in her early sixties, 'got up from a sick-bed to rescue a man from drowning in a rough sea', for which she received an award from the Royal Humane Society, but not, apparently, its premier award. Woodward, thinking this unjust, wrote to the Society asking for the award to be upgraded, and was angry when told that the grade having been announced it could not be changed. Her son believed that it was this incident which was responsible for Woodward's decision to make Violet Horsfall the chief beneficiary of his will. James Horsfall recalled staying with 'Uncle George' at Highgate when travelling from his home in Suffolk to his school. He remembered Woodward as being 'big, strong, and athletic' even in old-age, and of his always wearing the cassock, in London as in Highgate He remembered him playing the Bechstein concert grand piano in the drawing room, and attending to his bees in the garden; how he drank Marsala at dinner every evening, and how he still went regularly to the British Museum reading room. Of how, too, he seemed dour and rarely to smile, and yet beneath the stern exterior there was the twinkling of a keen yet dry sense of humour. He also remembered an occasion when 'one hot summers evening walking to the village he suddenly started spitting lightly on the ground. "I am afraid you have swallowed a fly" I said. "No dear boy" he replied "we are just passing the Chapel and I am purifying the ground".'[13] Today this attitude towards another Christian denomination seems surprising, but such intolerance would not have been unusual in a devout and conservative Anglo-catholic of this period. In his 1916 sermon at Beckenham he had been similarly dismissive of Roman Catholicism, refer-ring to the Roman Catholic Church as 'a corrupt following of the Apostle'.

It is not clear who else Woodward saw and corresponded with during the last few years of his life. Some of his friends and contemporaries were dead, as he recalled in his autobio-graphical notes, whilst others were living in different parts of the country and may have rarely visited London; Goldsmith, for example, was in Devon. One friend who certainly was in contact with him at this time, however, was Athelstan Riley, ten years his junior, and the author of the brief memoir which appeared in the late nineteen-thirties. Riley and Woodward shared not only an adherence to a rigid and devout form of Anglo-catholicism, but also an interest in Orthodoxy and in hymnology. Riley had published a book *Birkbeck and the Russian Church* in 1917, and had made an extensive 'Greek Orthodox' expedition in 1923.[14] He was also one the compilers of *The English Hymnal*, to which he contributed his well-known composition 'Ye Watchers and Ye Holy Ones', together with his translation from the Latin 'O Food of Men Wayfaring'. Riley, who like Birkbeck possessed both wealth and taste, had lived on Jersey since 1912 at the beau-tiful house he had built there, Trinity Manor; nevertheless he retained a house at Little Petherick in Cornwall, where he spent a part of each year. His diary for 1931 contains notes on how to get to Highgate village by public transport,[15] and this strongly suggests that he visited Woodward at West Hill. His papers in the Lambeth Palace Library also contain a single letter from Woodward, written on January 27th 1930. This contains a few items of news, and reference to Lord Grey having split with Lloyd George because he believed it was a 'doubtful matter' as to whether England should have dealings with the Soviet government. Woodward, with his life-long hatred of all kinds of liberalism and of oppression was incensed by this, and hoped that Grey's 'doubts' might be removed by his coming to learn the facts about Bolshevic atrocities. 'But', he added, 'being a Radical, like all the rest of them, pig-headed and whig-headed, they put their pet policies before religion, & Christ: & forget their old way of liberty, equality & fraternity. When will the tyranny in Russia end.'[16] Riley, having written as early as 1884 'I am an anti-liberal ("Conservative" or "Tory" do not express what I mean, being mere party names) simply because I am a Christian man; and I have never yet known a man with really Liberal principles who was *thoroughly* sound on matters of faith',[17] would doubtless have been in full agreement. But good-humour was never far away, and the letter closed with a typically whimsical Woodward joke: 'I hope you had a smooth, & not *sic transit* from St Helier'.

According to James Horsfall, Woodward often spoke about the parish church at Walsingham during these last years, and it seems that the Norfolk parish where he had ministered half-a-century earlier had always had a special place in his affections. It had found mention in his ballad *Cock Robin and Jenny Wren* in 1911, and again in a rather curious item which found inclusion in *The Cambridge Carol Book* of 1924:

> I was, and am,
> And ay shall be sad-hearted
> For Walsingham,
> To see her day departed:
>
> Her minster walls and stalls o'erthown,
> Her cells and wells with moss o'ergrown:
> Above her own, were stood the throne
> Of Mary's Son, Lo! ne'er a stone.[18]

These words echo, most probably unknowingly, the words of the sixteenth-century lament *In the Wrackes of Walsingham*, which exists in manuscript form in the Bodleian Library at Oxford, and has been attributed to Philip, Earl of Arundel.[19] If Woodward wrote them maybe a couple of years before their publication in 1924, then ironically they were composed just at the time when a new 'day' was dawning for Walsingham, following the appointment of The Revd Alfred

Hope Patten as Vicar. Fr Patten, born in 1885 (during Woodward's own incumbency) had in 1922 set up an image of Our Lady of Walsingham in a side-chapel of the Parish Church, had instituted daily 'Shrine Prayers', and had set upon the course of reviving the devotion, a course which would lead to Walsingham becoming once again a renowned centre of pilgrimage. It was a development of which Woodward himself seems to have approved, since according to his Obituary in the *Eastern Daily Press* he became 'one of the priest associates of the Holy House when the Shrine of Our Lady of Walsingham was rebuilt in 1931, and he made a pilgrimage to the shrine in 1932'. The circumstances of this pilgrimage remain unknown. The Holy House and the first section of the present Shrine Church were indeed built in 1931 (in which year Niall Campbell, Duke of Argyll, who was by this time Patron of the Plainsong and Mediaeval Music Society, became one of the first Guardians of the Holy House), but the body of Priest Associates had been instituted in 1927.[19] That Woodward joined them at this earlier date, and was eager to identify himself with what was taking place at Walsingham, is maybe indicated by the fact that in 1928 he describes himself as 'Sometime Vicar of Walsingham' on the title pages of five out of the six booklets which he printed during that year.[20] His expressed wish that the Virgin Mary should be honoured as a safeguard to the doctrine of the Incarnation, and his personal devotion to the Mother of God which seems to have been encouraged by his involvement with the devotional literature of the Orthodox Church, would certainly have made him sympathetic to the restoration of Marian devotion in the Church of England. There is no evidence that Woodward himself encouraged such devotion at Walsingham during his own incumbency, but insofar as he introduced the Anglo-catholic revival to the parish, he may be seen as having prepared the way for the work which Fr Patten, with his particular gifts of imagination and determination, later accomplished. The importance of this preparatory work – not least in possibly having encouraged Fr Patten to accept the living – should probably not be underestimated. Woodward's continuing interest in Walsingham may be seen too in the bequest of one hundred pounds 'to be spent upon the Church of the Parish'.

Woodward left a similar sum to St Augustine's Highgate, the church where, as he wrote in the letter to Violet Horsfall on October 16th 1929 'I have given my help (such as it was) for the last 14 years'. He had remained faithful to St Augustine's even during the years 1923 to 1929, when his friend and former colleague at the Berkeley Chapel and St Mark's Marylebone, James Adderley, had been incumbent of St Anne's Highgate, which lies just at the bottom of West Hill. Latterly he was taken to church by motor car; in an undated letter to Violet Horsfall which was clearly written in the late 1920s, and which he signs 'Your ever affectionate old Uncle', he speaks of 'a good natured, Catholic-minded lady, and a Scot Jacobite, who drives me in her motor-car, 'Betsey' its name, to & from S.Augustine's, Archway Road: for I find the hill trying to my old British Constitution: but 10 years ago I thought nothing of it.' Several ladies in fact seem to have assisted him in this way, because in his final letter of instruction, written a few months before his death, he told his executrix 'Holder will give you the names & addresses of about 8 young ladies, who have for several years past been kind enough to give me a lift in their motor-cars to & from St Augustine's, at all hours of the day, early and late, in winter and summer, fair and foul weather. Perhaps you would choose for these eight Arundel Society Pictures, as a keep sake from me.' He was clearly held in great affection at St Augustine's, because after his death a very handsome memorial was erected to him by subscription. Appropriately in view of his devotion to the Blessed Virgin Mary, this took the form of a large stone statue of Our Lady placed within the west portal of the church, and flanked by a commemorative inscription carved in low relief.[21]

James Horsfall recalled that his great-step-uncle remained in fairly good health until the last few months of his life, despite the inevitable weakening which age brought to his 'old British Constitution'. Clearly there were times when he was unwell, and written on the envelope of the first letter of instruction to Violet Horsfall – probably by Miss Holder – are the words 'Given to me on Oct. 10th 1929 when Dr

Woodward felt poorly'. This does not quite accord with the letter itself, which is dated October 16th. The letter began 'In order to simplify your work, as my sole Executrix, the following bits of information ought to be given you, during my life-time ...', after which he proceeded to give various pieces of information and instruction, starting in a business-like way by saying that a certain undertaker is to be used, who is to 'do that for my body which was done for so many of my best & oldest friends at St Barnabas'. He says that 'the Vicar of Walsingham (the Revd Hope Paten [sic]) has promised to bury me side by side with Dear Alice, in the Walsingham Churchyard. But I hope they will sing a Requiem for me at St Augustine's Church, near here.' He says of his house 'You may sell or keep this house, as you please ... If it be put up for sale, my neighbour Mr Cloutman, ought to have first refusal, for he owns Admiral Sir H. Purey-Cust's house next door, & would like to throw this and that into one.' In the event the Horsfall family retained the house, and it was the home of Violet's son James until his death in 1988.

At the conclusion of his memoir Athelstan Riley wrote 'towards the end of 1933 it was clear that he was failing', and this statement is verified by the second and final letter of instruction, which is dated November 3th 1933 and written in a smaller and less legible hand than he had used in the past. He speaks of Miss Holder as 'doing her utmost to prolong my days on earth', but adding that 'these are already numbered'. He reiterates the funeral arrangements, saying that 'After my death, Fr Hodgson has promised to sing Vespers of the Dead for me at St Augustine's Highgate & to sing a Requiem for me the next morning. After which will follow the committal of my earthly remains at Walsingham, that same afternoon, and where the present Vicar has promised me room in or next dear Alice's grave'. He added to the letter on November 8th, saying:

> I have not forgotten my faithful servant in my will, but there are several little things which also I bequeathe her; such as my <u>Excelsior Press</u> on <u>the top stair case landing</u>, together with all my type (Point no. 8) with furniture to match. I have also written her name in several books, especially in <u>birds and</u>

gardens, also a copper preserving bowl: also a book-binding machine in the kitchen.

After certain other directions, he added:

> My bee-appliances do as you think advisable with them. Perhaps Jimmy, or Ronald, would find them useful. My new Oxford English Dictionary is now complete, and very valuable! Keep it for yourself. XII or XIII large vols. The same with any of my books. Any that you don't care for might be offered to the Cowley Fathers, or to Kelham Theological College, or the like.

After which – like his father towards the end of his life – he wrote about the state of some of his investments, before concluding 'Come here when equal to the journey & cheer me up with your presence. Holder will make you comfortable. Ever your loving Uncle, George R. Woodward'.

Perhaps he rallied somewhat in the new year, because Riley asserts that 'within a few weeks of his end he managed to celebrate the Holy Mysteries at the altar of St Augustine's, Highgate'. But his days, as he said, 'were already numbered', and he died on Saturday March 3rd, 1934, 'strengthened for his entry into the Unseen by the last Sacraments', and having reached the age of eighty-six.

The funeral rites, which followed the pattern he had requested, began at St Augustine's on Tuesday March 6th, and were reported in the *Church Times* on the following Friday. According to the report,

> On Tuesday evening the body was taken to the church of St Augustine's, Highgate, where the Office of Vespers for the Dead was sung. On Wednesday morning, three Low Masses of Requiem were said for the repose of his soul. At eleven o'clock, a large congregation attended the solemn Requiem, at which the celebrant was the Vicar, the Revd J. H Hodgson. The Proper of the Mass was sung to the traditional Plainchant, and the Absolutions to the setting of Viadana. '*De Profundis Exclamantes*' (350 English Hymnal) was the Offertory hymn. Between the Mass and the Absolutions, Bach's prelude '*Liebster Jesu*', for which Dr Woodward had a great affection, was played by Mr C. A. James, organist of the church. Many priests came to render their last tribute to their brother, and not a few laymen. In the clergy stalls was Canon Hallett, Warden of the House of Mercy, Highgate. The beautiful

church formed an ideal setting for such a service, with its solemn ritual and devout congregation, holding lighted candles at the Gospel, the Canon, and the Absolutions. The coffin rested on a catafalque in the nave, and was covered with a pall, on which Dr Woodward's birreta was placed. Many flowers had been sent, and surrounded the bier, which was flanked on either side by tapers of unbleached wax.

The body was then conveyed by road to Walsingham, to be buried in the place where the body of his wife, Alice, had been laid to rest forty years previously. Clearly Walsingham and its Incumbent, Fr A. H. Patten, were not to be outdone by the solemnity of the rites which had already taken place at Highgate, as an account in the *Eastern Daily Press*, published on the same day as that in the *Church Times*, makes clear. On arrival at Walsingham, the body _

> ... was met at the church by the clergy of the parish, accompanied by Crucifix and lights. The coffin was sprinkled with holy water and borne into the chancel where it was placed between the six tall funeral lights. Vespers, Matins, and Lauds of the Dead were then said. On Thursday morning being the Feast of St Felix, the Apostle of East Anglia, there was a sung Mass of the feast at eight o'clock, and at 11 o'clock a Solemn Requiem Mass was sung, followed by the Absolutions. At two o'clock the choir and clergy took their places in the stalls and the funeral service was sung, at the conclusion of which the body was borne to the grave, attended by the priests and choir monotoning the antiphon 'May the Angels lead thee unto Paradise' and psalms for the repose of the soul. At the same time the 'Dead March' was played on the organ by Mr George Back, organist of St Mary's. With the one exception all the services, Mass and burial were unaccompanied and sung to plain song. After the committal the coffin was again sprinkled with holy water. The choir retired to the church reciting Psalms for the Dead.

The mourners at Walsingham, led by Violet Horsfall, her husband, and son James, included Woodward's faithful housekeeper Miss Holder, together with a number of local clergy and parishioners. Henry Lee Warner – the last of his name to live at Walsingham Abbey – having died in 1916, the only mention of Woodward's wife's family in the newspaper account is of Mrs J. Blake-Humphrey, a Lee Warner connection, who attended the funeral and represented 'Miss Lee

Warner, of Holt', presumably one of the sisters whom he had known half a century earlier at 'Lohengrin Lodge'.

Strangely, the exact location of Woodward's burial place is now unknown. Whilst he had said in his directions of November 1933 that he hoped to be buried 'in or near dear Alice's grave', those dating from 1929 had said he wished to be buried 'side by side' with her, and in the will which he made in 1932 he gave directions for a separate gravestone to be erected. These things, together with the facts that no additional inscription was added to his wife's memorial, and that the writer of the 'Appreciation' in the *Eastern Daily Press* wrote of his having been buried by the side of his wife, imply that he occupies a separate grave. As regards his gravestone, he had specified in his will that 'I desire if possible to be buried in Little Walsingham Churchyard and on the recumbent Cross over my grave it shall suffice to have the following inscription thus and no more 'Sub signo tau Georgius Ratcliffe Woodward Sacerdos indignus'.[22] Presumably this memorial, impressive in its simplicity, was put in place, but if so it was lost when a large number of grave-stones were removed and destroyed in the late nineteen-sixties or early nineteen-seventies, presumably in the interests of easy grass-cutting. No record of the position of the graves was kept, and Woodward remained uncommemorated in Walsingham until 1982, when a mural-tablet was placed in a side-chapel of St Mary's to mark the centenary of his coming to the parish. Around the edge of this tablet are inscribed words from his carol 'This Joyful Eastertide':

> My flesh in hope shall rest,
> And for a season slumber:
> Till trump from east to west
> Shall wake the dead in number.[23]

The side-chapel, dedicated to St Catherine and lying on the south side of the church, is flooded with the light which comes in through the clear glass of its large windows, and beyond them lies the churchyard where Woodward, surrounded by the remains of those to whom he once minis-tered, is buried. There, far from the rush and noise of London, in a place where the only sounds are those of the stirring of the breeze in the long grasses and the distant singing of pilgrims, his mortal remains await the General Resurrection for which he hoped, and which he had celebrated in one of his best-known carols.

# CONCLUSION

The liturgical scholar Dom Gregory Dix wrote memorably of Woodward's friend and associate Bishop Walter Frere that 'there were in him three men, the ecclesiastical statesman, the scholar and the man of God.'[1] The same kind of judgement could not be made accurately of Woodward, for whilst it is true that three things – priesthood, poetry, and music – were particularly important in his life, these things were completely interdependent. So that there were not three men in him, but rather one man, who was first and foremost a priest in the catholic tradition of Christendom, and who felt that his distinctive work and mission as an ecclesiastic was to enrich the choral music of the Church by making available fine tunes accompanied by well-matched words. Perhaps the essential unity of his of life as priest, poet, and musician was to some degree expressed by he title he bore during his second curacy at St Barnabas' Pimlico – that of Precentor: the priest in an ecclesiastical establishment who is responsible for the excellence of what is sung.

Yet unified though the priest, poet, and musician were in Woodward, it is still helpful to consider his work in each of the three particular areas, and to assess the gifts and skills which he brought to them individually. As priest, Athelstan Riley called him 'a pious ecclesiastic who never forgot, nor allowed others to forget, his priestly office', and outwardly his complete commitment to priesthood was clearly expressed by his constant wearing of the cassock, as it was too by his regular and frequent participation in worship. He was emphatically not one of those scholar-clergymen whose academic interests seem paramount, and whose priesthood seems incidental. It is true of course that he spent only twelve years as a parish priest, and that after he left St Mark's Marylebone in 1904 at the age of fifty-six he held no further parochial appointment. But it would be wrong to see this as some kind of escape from parish work, or as an admission of failure in pastoral ministry. Rather he seems to have felt that he could best serve the Church by exercising his

musical and literary gifts, and that there was no contra-
diction between this activity and his priestly vocation. He
was not by temperament or calling the kind of outstanding
extravert that his friend and colleague James Adderley was;
he was not, it seems, a particularly distinguished preacher,
nor did he have the opportunity which W. J. E. Bennett had
to show himself a confessor of the faith by undergoing persecution. Again, there is no evidence to suggest that he was in
particular demand as a director of souls, nor that he had any
outstanding gift of spiritual discernment. But it is not neces-
sarily the possession of such special or unusual gifts and
charisms which give a priest distinction. The devotion and
diligence and single-mindedness of a priest 'who never
forgot, nor allowed others to forget, his priestly office' is not
negligible, and neither of course is that happy ability to win
the lasting affection of the people to whom he ministers.
There is very clear evidence from Walsingham, Pimlico, and
Highgate that Woodward possessed this latter gift. Certainly
the priesthood to which he believed he had been called was
fundamental to the life he led, and he unquestionably finds a
place amongst those learned, devout, and disciplined priests
who were one of the finest fruits of the Anglo-catholic revival
in the Church of England.

It is more difficult to estimate Woodward's role as a poet.
He claimed at one time only to write verses to furnish certain
'fine old tunes' with words, but the fact that his output of
poetry was considerable – verses to be sung as hymns and
carols, longer narrative poems, the translation and rhyming
of epigrams – means that the composition of poetry played a
significant part in his life, and consequently that he must be
considered as a poet, whether good or bad. The temptation is
not to take his poetry seriously; to see and to dismiss the bulk
of it as being merely quaint, awkward, forced, and ultimately
unworthy of either serious consideration or preservation,
whilst maintaining that such words as those of 'Ding Dong!
Merrily on High' are only tolerable because, as Mervyn
Horder put it, they have been 'swept by their bouncing
French tune into universal currency'.[2] Yet it would clearly be
unfair to judge the whole of Woodward's poetic output by
the worst examples of it. Some pieces that he wrote certainly

are mundane almost to the point of banality. He probably wrote and published far too many verses, and this most particularly when he was seeking to provide words for so many of the tunes which he wanted to include in *The Cowley Carol Book*, *Songs of Syon*, *An Italian Carol Book*, and *The Cambridge Carol Book*. In these cases he was working under considerable pressure, and it was almost inevitable that he would produce at least some words which were less than felicitous. Again, the matter of fashion must be recognised. His style and choice of word and phrase must have seemed old-fashioned even when first produced in the early part of the century – indeed he often intended it to be so, for reasons which he openly stated – and so it is not surprising that they seem the more so now. Yet his poetry has not been without its admirers. Alfred Gurney, a man of some literary taste, considered that his verse translations had 'a touch of genius', Sir William Hadow writing to Archbishop Davidson spoke of his 'poetic powers of the highest kind', and according to Athelstan Riley the Poet Laureate, Robert Bridges, had 'a high opinion of his work'. Nevertheless it could not be argued that Woodward was a considerable poet: in his verse there is a paucity of original and striking imagery, a lack of smooth and seemingly-effortless expression, with a limitation of vocabulary (most noticeable in the words which he rhymes), which together make his poetry for the most part less than memorable. And yet there are undeniably individual pieces which have considerable charm and which perhaps deserve to be better known.

What then of Woodward the musician? It is important first of all to be clear as to the scope of Woodward's contribution to this field. Dom Anslem Hughes referred to him as 'a musician of no little ability and fastidious taste, both as a composer and as an executant'.[3] It is true that Woodward played the euphonium, the piano, the 'cello, and possibly other instruments too, and also that his knowledge of musical history and theory seem to have been very extensive. But it is rather misleading to speak of him as a composer. His 'compositions' seem to have been limited to the considerable number of harmonisations which he prepared for his various collections of hymns and carols, and whilst this might seem a

small field to have worked in, his work within it has nevertheless won considerable praise from musicians. Dr Roy
Massey, for example, the Organist of Hereford Cathedral
and a conductor of the Three Choirs Festival has spoken of
Woodward's     harmonisations     as     being     'astonishingly
assured', adding that 'he responded unerringly to the
harmonic implications of the melody, producing lower parts
which were models of their kind – absolutely grammatical,
transparent of texture, and never swamping the simple
melodies with over-elaborate harmonic movement. His
harmonies have an inevitability about them which compares
favourably with those of Charles Wood and Ralph Vaughan
Williams who were similarly masters of their craft in this
same area.'[4] Woodward often seems to have been confused
(and many would say to his detriment) with the Revd H. H.
Woodward who became Precentor of Worcester Cathedral in
1890, and who composed a number of chants, together with
a setting for the Holy Communion Service.[5] No such compositions seem to have come from G. R. Woodward's hand.

Woodward's real significance as a musician lies in the
hymn and carol collections which he made and published,
and it will be remembered that it was this work which was
cited by Walford Davies and Hadow when urging Davidson
to bestow the honorary doctorate of music upon him. In
these collections, and most especially in *The Cowley Carol
Book* and in *Songs of Syon* he collected and brought before
the musical public a very large number of fine tunes which
had lain neglected for too long, and his work in resurrecting
and making available tunes which had been lost in old books
and manuscripts may perhaps be seen as some sort of parallel
to the work of rescuing and making-known folk-tunes which
others were engaged in at about the same time. It is true that
the collections which Woodward produced are now little
used themselves, and yet many church musicians continue to
speak of them in the way that Kenneth Long did of *Songs of
Syon* when he called it 'an important source book' which has
been 'drawn on by most subsequent compilers'.[6] In his
collections, and not least in the part which *The Cowley Carol
Book* played in popularising carols in the earlier part of this
century, Woodward certainly made a significant contribution

to English church music, whilst his quiet contribution to the revival and promotion of Plainsong, made over so many years, must also be remembered although here his work was overshadowed by that of his friends G. H. Palmer and W. H. Frere.

It would be unrealistic and unhelpful to exaggerate Woodward's gifts and achievements, whether as priest, poet or musician. In each of these fields his abilities were very real, but so too were his limitations. Perhaps, however, his true distinction should not be sought in outward achievement, but rather in the kind of person whom he was – that is in his essential character. His friend Athelstan Riley considered that this was something of which it was 'difficult to convey an impression to those who did not know him', and of which Edward Wood spoke when he recalled Woodward as being an 'impressively "Good" ' man. What were the main elements which distinguished Woodward's character? Self-discipline was certainly one of them, that self-discipline which was so admired and commended by the particular religious movement in which Woodward had his roots and which more than anything else made him the person that he was. Self-discipline not just in the ordered practice of the spiritual life, although that was fundamental, but also in the moral life which was founded upon it. Perhaps in Woodward this is seen most obviously in that characteristic gentleness which various people remarked upon, and which was most likely present in him not by nature but only by the rigid exercise of self-discipline. By nature he may well have been somewhat aggressive, wilful, and impatient, attributes which are suggested by the surviving photograph of him as a young man. Riley remembered that if his strong principles were 'touched in the slightest degree in any company he would flame forth in a brief burst of fury which astounded his hearers who had known him only in his habitual gentleness'. This certainly suggests that his 'habitual gentleness' was achieved by the exercise of self-discipline, a discipline which, because he was human, occasionally broke down. Yet if his gentleness was not achieved without an effort of will, his characteristic humility would seem to have been primarily a gift of nature. The writer of 'A Funeral Tribute' in the

*Eastern Daily Press* remembered his having been 'entirely without worldly ambition', whilst his telling Archbishop Davidson in 1924 that he would have been 'quite content to go plodding away without notice' has the ring of sincerity. It is consonant too with his having been content to return to the status of an assistant curate in 1894 after having held two incumbencies, and with his choice of the words 'unworthy priest' for the inscription of his gravestone. This humility, like the gentleness and self-discipline which also characterised him, is typical of the best products of the spirituality of the Anglo-catholic revival, and unites him with such men as John Keble and Edward King.

Another element in Woodward's character was loyalty. On the surface, his intense and life-long loyalty to his school and to his college is very apparent, not least in the 1924 letter to Davidson and the 1927 speech at Gonville and Caius. It took him year after year to the Eton and Harrow match at Lords, and also it seems to the annual Boat Race, and to the Henley Regatta. But on a deeper level there was his loyal and unswerving admiration of the work of John Mason Neale, which he had first come to know as an undergraduate at Cambridge, and of which he was still writing appreciatively nearly sixty years later. Most of all however there was his complete loyalty to the revealed truth of the Christian Faith. Several writers have remarked on his unshakeable 'principles', and in a number of the Prefaces he wrote he urged the need to stand by the truths which the Church has both received and given witness to down the ages. To some, this loyal upholding of traditional Christian teaching, coupled with a hearty dislike and suspicion of theological speculation, opens him to the charge of narrowness and even bigotry; but others would join Riley in admiring the fact that Woodward would 'never make terms with anything he thought wrong, or give way an inch where his convictions were at stake; he was true to himself and true to his God'. Linked with this loyalty to the truth was the uncompromising love of excellence which is seen writ large in the collections of hymns and carols which he made, and writ small in the booklets he wrote and printed during his last years. Thoughts of success, commercial or otherwise, were always quite secondary to this prime concern; he wished to set and to achieve high musical and literary standards, and whether others would follow where he tried to lead was not of the first importance. In his work he was a perfectionist, and the perfectionist in his or her more hidden way is every bit as important and as necessary as the popularist. As the writer of 'An Appreciation', which likewise appeared in the *Eastern Daily Press* at the time of Woodward's death, maintained 'There is also a place of honour for those who stand out for the highest, whether in religion, morals, or music, and set up a standard for others to look up to when faint of heart'.[7] With his characteristic gentleness, humility, self-discipline, loyalty, love of excellence, and complete integrity it may be that George Ratcliffe Woodward both represents a standard for the Christian of today, and also deserves to be remembered not only for what he achieved, but for the person he was.

# NOTES

## Chapter 1: The Early Years 1848–1868

1. The *Cambridge Carol Book*, ed. Charles Wood and G. R. Woodward, London, 1924, p. 6.
2. Ibid., p. 7.
3. These Notes, referred to in Sources, must have been written after 1925, since reference is made to the Mersey Tunnel which was begun in that year, and completed in 1933. Again a late date is suggested by the fact that he speaks of many of his contemporaries at preparatory school having already died.
4. Besford Court was successively home of the Besford, Harewell, and Sebright families. It does not appear to have belonged to any Woodwards. Arley Castle was bought by one Robert Woodward in 1852, and Woodwards appear to have remained there until 1952. It is just possible that this Robert Woodward may have been the brother of G. R. W.'s grandfather. Bricklehampton Hall was built in 1848 by a Woodward, who left it some years later. Information from *Burke's and Savills Guide to Country Houses Vol. 2*, London, 1980, pps. 192, 193 & 195. These Worcestershire Woodwards are likely to have been at most fairly distant relations of G. R. W.
5. G. R. W. possessed a portrait of this Jonathan Ratcliffe. In his will, proved on April 12th 1934, he left it to Basil Ratcliffe Woodward, his nephew, together with 'the old Grandfather Clock in my Hall', presumably another family heirloom.
6. Recorded in the Baptismal Register of St Nicholas' Church, Liverpool, Entry No. 1839, now deposited in the Liverpool Record Office, City Library, Liverpool.
7. Athelstan Riley's appreciation, described in Sources, is undated. However the late Mr James Horsfall, son of G. R. W.'s step-niece and heir Violet Horsfall, had in his possession a letter from Riley concerning the appreciation which was dated May 19th 1938, indicating that it was being compiled at that time, four years after G. R. W.'s death.
8. G. L. Prestige, *The Life of Charles Gore*, London, 1935, p. 6.
9. V. H. Stanton on Westcott in *The Dictionary of National Biography, Second Supplement, Vol. 3*, London, 1912, p. 636.
10. This was asserted in the anonymous Obituary which appeared in the *Church Times* on March 9th 1934.
11. Bernaar Rainbow on Farmer in *The New Grove Dictionary of Music and Musicians, Vol. 6*, ed. Stanley Sadie, London, 1980, p. 402. John Farmer taught at Harrow 1862–1885, becoming Organist at Balliol College Oxford in the latter year.
12. This letter, dated March 21st 1924, is preserved in the Davidson papers, Lambeth Palace Library.
13. G. L. Prestige, Op. cit., p. 9.
14. Quoted in G. K. A. Bell, *Randall Davidson, Archbishop of Canterbury, Vol. 1*, London, 1935, p. 16.
15. See *The Dictionary of National Biography 1922–1930*, Oxford, 1937, pps. 495–7.

## Chapter Two: Cambridge and Pimlico 1869–1882

1. John Venn *Biographical History of Gonville and Caius College Cambridge, Vol. 2*, Cambridge, 1898, p. 382.
2. G. L. Prestige, Op. Cit., p. 8.
3. See C. G. Griffinhoofe *The Story of S.T.C.*, Cambridge, 1915.
4. See Peter Anson *Fashions in Church Furnishings 1840–1850*, London, 1960, pps. 44–74.
5. G. R. Woodward *The Most Holy Mother of God in the Songs of the Eastern Church*, London, 1919, p. 8.
6. Quoted by Ian Copley *The Music of Charles Wood – A Critical Study*, London, 1978, p. 183.
7. This letter, together with those written to G. R. W. by his father and quoted in this and the following chapter, are all in the possession of his great-great-step-niece, Mrs Ann Duff.
8. See Ken Powell 'Popery in Pimlico', in *County Life*, Nov. 14th, 1985, p. 1502.
9. Ibid.
10. Quoted in *The History of St Barnabas', Pimlico*, Anon., London, 1933, p. 36.
11. Ibid. p. 36.
12. See *Historical Companion to Hymns Ancient and Modern*, Ed. Maurice Frost, London, 1962, p. 119.
13. *The History of St Barnabas'*, p. 37.
14. James Horsfall recalled that Basil Woodward had specialised in drawing caricatures; the reference in this letter to his fiddle is the only indication that he may have shared his elder brother's interest in music.

## Chapter Three: Walsingham 1882–1888

1. Great, or Old, Walsingham was not then joined ecclesiastically to Little Walsingham and Houghton St Giles' as it is now. Little Walsingham was, and is, the main village, the epithets Great and Little referring to the acreage of the settlements rather than to their comparative population.
2. For the history of the mediaeval shrine see Colin Stephenson *Walsingham Way*, London, 1970, pps. 17–54.
3. See Edward Lee Warner *The Life of John Warner, Bishop of Rochester 1637–1666 with Appendix Containing some Account of his Successors, the Lee Warner Family*, London, 1901.
4. Colin Stephenson Op. Cit., pps. 77–8.
5. Ibid., p. 77.
6. See Rose Katherine Birkbeck *Life and Letters of W. J. Birkbeck by his Wife*, London, 1922, p. 86.
7. Martin had only moved to the adjacent parish of East Barsham, which he held with nearby Little Snoring. His Preachers' Book remains in the parish records at Walsingham.
8. *Lynn Advertiser*, October 14th 1882, p. 5.
9. See Owen Chadwick *The Victorian Church, Part 1*, London, 1966, p. 517.
10. The Service Register of the period, preserved in the parish records at Walsingham, records collections on behalf of all three of these societies.
11. Colin Stephenson asserts that G. R. W. placed six candles on the High Altar, but provides no evidence for this. Op. Cit., p. 78.

12. This Log Book, which gives a very full picture of the impact of the Anglo-catholic revival on a small country parish in the 1880s, deserves to be better known. It too is preserved in the parish records at Walsingham.
13. See *The History of St Barnabas, Pimlico*, p. 26.
14. A few years later G. R. W. would have disapproved of this book, which favours the Mechlin use; the plainsong pioneered by Solesmes came to be recognised as more authentic. See Hilda Andrews *Westminster Retrospect, A Memoir of Sir Richard Terry*, Oxford, 1948, Chs. 2 & 3.
15. Dom Anslem Hughes *Septuagesima*, London, 1959, p. 27.
16. *Lynn Advertier* May 5th, 1883 p. 5.
17. Ibid., November 4th, 1882, p. 5.
18. Ibid., January 13th, 1883, p. 5.
19. Ibid., August 18th, 1883, p. 5.
20. Ibid., May 3rd, 1884, p. 5.
21. 'Ding Dong! Merrily on High' first appeared in a booklet called *Carols for Yule-tide* which G. R. W. compiled and printed in 1922. In the index it was entitled 'Ding Dong! Merrily the Bells'. In the same booklet was another carol composed by him, and not subsequently reprinted, called 'Six We Be in Number, Each a Minster Bell'.
22. *Lynn Advertiser*, April 19th 1884, p. 5.
23. G. R. Woodward *Hymns of the Greek Church*, London, 1922, p. 14.
24. Hilda Andrews, Op. Cit., p. 70.
25. *Lynn Advertiser*, October 6th 1888, p. 3.
26. Ibid., January 13th 1883, p. 5.
27. Rose Katherine Birkbeck, Op. Cit., Preface p. VIII.
28. It is possible that Hughes may be mistaken in asserting that G. R. W. played the 'cello at or after the daily choral evensongs at Walsingham; the performer may well have been Henry Lee Warner, the son of his Patron. Sir Laurence Jones in the first volume of his autobiography *A Victorian Boyhood*, London, 1935, wrote of Henry Lee Warner 'He lunched at four o'clock in the afternoon; and afterwards strolled across to the church to play the 'cello at the daily evening-service', pps. 44–45.
29. Chandos Lee Warner, who became G. R. W.'s brother-in-law, married Lady Dorothea Augusta Fitzclarence, daughter of the Earl of Munster. He lived at Tyberton Court, the Lee Warner home in Herefordshire, and in 1916 inherited the Walsingham estate on the death of the unmarried Henry Lee Warner. The Walsingham estate was heavily mortgaged by then, and was sold to Sir Eustace Gurney, whose wife, Agatha, was a grand-daughter of Canon Henry James Lee Warner.
30. *Lynn Advertiser*, February 9th 1884, p. 5.
31. Ibid, April 19th, 1884, p. 5.
32. Charles Wood Mss, Gonville and Caius College Library, Cambridge. Letter dated December 20th 1926.
33. *Lynn Advertiser*, January 5th, 1889, p. 5.

## Chapter Four: Chelmondiston 1888–1894

1. Colin Stephenson, Op. Cit., p. 78.
2. For information concerning the founding of the Plainsong and Mediaeval Music Society see Anselm Hughes, Op. Cit., pps. 13–14.

3. G. R. Woodward *A Sermon (on Matthew XXV.40) preached at St Barnabas', Pimlico, July 15th 1900*, London, 1900, p. 6.
4. Quoted by Gavin Stamp and Anthony Symondson in *Clumber Chapel*, London, 1982, p. 23.
5. See the Faculty in the Suffolk Record Office, Ipswich, and the guide book to Chelmondiston Church by Roy Tricker, 1990.
6. The book is Charles Boutell *Monumental Brasses and Slabs*, London, 1847. It is inscribed 'To James Dagless from The Revd G. R. Woodward. A small token of great regard. Walsingham, Dec. 31st 1888'. On the opposite page, written in pencil, is 'G. R. Woodward. 5 Chester Terrace SW'. Perhaps this is where G. R. W. lived during his curacy at St Barnabas', Pimlico, 1874–1882. Opposite p. 118 is an illustration of a brass monumental cross at Broadwater, Sussex, which was copied exactly at Walsingham for the memorial to Henry James Lee Warner, who died in 1886, and his wife Ellen Rosetta. It seems likely that G. R. W. had a hand in this. The brass survived the fire of 1961. It may be relevant that St Barnabas' had a number of fine monumental brasses. The book was given to the present writer by the grandaughter of James Dagless.
7. The 1894 Terrier is also in the Chelmondiston church records at The Suffolk Record Office, Ipswich.
8. See *The Sevenoaks Telegraph*, July 13th, 1889.
9. On the origin of carols see for example *The Oxford Book of Carols*, London, 1928, Preface, pps. vi-xii.
10. G. R. Woodward *Carols for Christmas-tide*, London, 1892, p. 13.
11. Ibid., p. 9.
12. See Hilda Andrews, Op. Cit., p. 147.
13. Charles Wood Mss, Gonville and Caius College Library, Cambridge.
14. See Ian Copley, Op. Cit., p. 32.
15. G. R. Woodward *Carols for Christmas-tide, Series II*, London, 1893, p. 15.
16. Ibid. p. 13.
17. This letter was discovered inside a second-hand book bought by Fr Graham Leonard, formerly Bishop of London, and is now in his possession. The book was *Magister Choralis: A Theoretical and Practical Manual of Gregorian Chant*, London, 1877. Written in the book is the name W. H. Sewell, who may have been the recipient of the letter.
18. Woodward frequently used this means of dating, as did other Anglo-catholics of the period. He may personally have derived the practice from J. M. Neale, who, for example, dated his *Carols for Christmas-tide* 'S. S. Simon and Jude, 1853'.
19. G. R. Woodward *Legends of the Saints*, London, 1898, p. 104.

## Chapter Five: London 1894–1901

1. Ken Powell, Op. Cit., p. 1502.
2. Ibid., p. 1504.
3. G. R. Woodward *Hymns and Carols for Christmas-tide*, London, 1897, Preface (the pages containing the Preface are unnumbered).
4. Ibid., p. 11.
5. Ibid., p. 38.
6. The copy of *Hymns and Carols for Christmas-tide* in the British Library contains only the words of the hymns and carols. The Preface implies that the tunes had been published separately, and that the harmonisations would follow in due course in a third booklet. It has

not been possible to ascertain whether or not this did appear, and if
so whether it contained Woodward's earliest published harmonisations.
7. G. R. Woodward *The Seven Sleepers of Ephesus*, London, 1902, p. 1.
8. See Anselm Hughes, Op. Cit., p. 27.
9. G. R. Woodward *Poemata*, London, 1903, p. 17. The tone of
pessimism and nostalgia in this poem is reminiscent of that in J. M.
Neale's 'A Song for the Times', which G. R. W. included in *The
Cambridge Carol Book*, London, 1924, p. 60.
10. Ibid., p. 61.
11. See J. M. Close, writing on G. H. Palmer in *The Dictionary of
National Biography, 1922–1930 Supplement*, London, 1937, p. 652.
12. Letter to the author, June 12th, 1995.
13. Letter to the author, April 26th, 1995.
14. G. R. Woodward *The Cowley Carol Book*, Complete Edition,
London, 1947, p. 51.
15. Ibid, *Second Series*, London, 1919, p. (iii).
16. Percy Dearmer *The Oxford Book of Carols*, London, 1928, p. vi.
17. C. S. Phillips *Hymnody Past and Present*, London, 1937, p. 241.
18. *The Cowley Carol Book*, 1947 Ed., p. 98.
19. *Crockford's Clerical Directory* 1931 states that Woodward was at St
Mark's Marylebone 1903–1906, and makes no reference to his
having served at the Berkeley Chapel, whereas *The Clergy List* 1912
states that he was at the Berkeley Chapel 1899–1900, and at St
Mark's 1901–1904. There is a clear discrepancy here. Probably *The
Clergy List* 1912 is the more likely to be correct, both because it was
compiled considerably nearer to the time, and because the dates
concur with the established movements of James Adderley.
20. James Adderley *In Slums and Society*, London, 1916, pps. 79 and 83.

## Chapter Six: London 1901–1916

1. Quoted by T. P. Stevens in *Father Adderley*, London, 1943, p. 45.
2. J. G. Adderley, Op. Cit., p. 112.
3. Ibid. p. 113.
4. T. P. Stevens, Op. Cit., p. 44.
5. G. R. Woodward *Songs of Syon*, London, 1904, Preface (the pages
containing the Preface are unnumbered).
6. Ibid.
7. Obituary, Anon., *Church Times*, March 9th 1934.
8. Kenneth R. Long *The Music of the English Church*, London, 1972, p.
401.
9. *Songs of Syon*, 3rd. Ed., London, 1910, p. iv.
10. Ibid., p. iii.
11. Ibid., p. iv.
12. 'Remember me, my God, for this: and spare me according to the
greatness of your mercy.' These words are the Vulgate translation of
Nehemiah, 13:22.
13. *Songs of Syon*, 3rd. Ed., 1910, p. i.
14. This letter, together with the other letters to G. R. W. mentioned later
in the chapter, are all in the possession of Mrs Ann Duff.
15. *Songs of Syon*, 3rd. Ed., 1910, p. 176.
16. Ibid., p. 219.
17. Ibid., p. 513.
18. Ibid., p. 561.

19. C. S. Phillips, Op. Cit., p. 241.
20. Anselm Hughes, Op. Cit., p. 27. John Wilson, formerly an officer of The Hymn Society, wrote in a letter to the author on September 29th 1981, 'As regards *Songs of Syon*, I find it a sort of high-brow dream book, to which one goes to look up a source now and again. I have never heard of a church that actually used the book for regular worship'.
21. V. N. G., 'A Funeral Tribute', *Eastern Daily Press*, March 9th, 1934.
22. *Church Times*, Obituary, as above.
23. Mervyn Horder, *Bulletin 164* of The Hymn Society, July 1985, p. 53.
24. G. R. Woodward *Piae Cantiones*, London, 1910, p. xxv.
25. Anselm Hughes, Op. Cit., p. 27.
26. *Piae Cantiones*, p. 206.
27. G. R. Woodward *Cock Robin and Jenny Wren. A Ballad for Children*, London, 1911, p. 10.
28. Ibid., p. 9.
29. G. R. Woodward *Golden Lays of Olden Days*, London, 1911, p. viii.
30. Ibid., p. ix.
31. Ibid., p. x.
32. *Songs of Syon*, 3rd Ed., 1910, p. i.
33. *St John Damascene. Barlaam and Joasaph*, Ed. G. R. Woodward and H. Mattingly, Loeb Classical Library, London, 1914, p. vii.
34. Only one of these letters is dated by the year; a few are datable by the mention of events, or by the postmark when the envelope has survived.

## Chapter Seven: Highgate 1916–1924

1. Quoted by Arthur Oswald in 'Hill Village of North London', *Country Life*, November 19th 1964, p. 1320.
2. Bevis Hillier *Young Betjeman*, London, 1988, p. 15.
3. Woodward paid £1,470 for the house. When he died in 1934 the net value of his estate was £10,615.13.8. For the last thirty years of his life he seems to have lived on the income from shares, etc. left to him by his father, together with some additional share-income in which he had a life interest, and which at his death reverted to the Lee Warner family. This would be supplemented by income from the royalties on his more popular publications. In his will he left the royalty rights on *The Cowley Carol Book*, *The Cambridge Carol Book*, and *An Italian Carol Book*, together with the copyright to *Songs of Syon*, to the widow of his friend Charles Wood.
4. There is a photograph of West Hill at is appeared in 1910 in Bevis Hillier, Op. Cit., plate 5.
5. John Betjeman *Summoned by Bells*, London, 1960, p. 5.
6. Manuscripts of these three sermons are in the possession of Mrs Ann Duff.
7. G. R. Woodward *A Sermon (on Matthew XXV.40) Preached at St Barnabas, Pimlico. July 15th 1900*. Privately printed, London, 1900, pps. 4–5.
8. Quoted by Katherine Birkbeck Op. Cit., p. vii. In the preface to *The Acathist Hymn*, Woodward thanks Lord Halifax for his 'more-than-great interest' in the work.
9. G. R. Woodward and W. J. Birkbeck *The Acathist Hymn of the Holy Orthodox Church in the Original Greek Text and done into English Verse*, London, 1917, p. iii.

10. Ibid., p. iv.
11. Ibid., p. 7.
12. G. R. Woodward *The Most Holy Mother of God in the Songs of the Eastern Church*, London, 1919, p. 8.
13. Ibid., p. 8.
14. Ibid., p. 7.
15. Ibid. p. 21.
16. Ibid. p. 30.
17. See, for example, C. S. Phillips *Walter Howard Frere*, London, 1947, p. 185–6.
18. G. R. Woodward *Saint George Meglomartyr. In twenty hymns of The Holy and Orthodox Eastern Church, Now First done into English Verse*, London, 1919, p. 2.
19. G. R. Woodward *Hymns of the Greek Church*, London, 1922, p. 1.
20. Ibid., p. 23.
21. This letter was in the possession of the late James Horsfall.
22. Ian Copley, Op. Cit., pps. 179–180.
23. Letter to the author, June 7th 1982.
24. G. R. Woodward and C. Wood *The Cambridge Carol Book, Being Fifty-two Songs for Christmas, Easter, and Other Seasons*, London, 1924, p. 8.
25. Mervyn Horder, Op. Cit., p. 52.
26. *The Cambridge Carol Book*, p. 26.
27. G. R. Woodward *Acta Sanctorum, Being XII Poems*, London, 1924, p. 40.
28. Ibid., p. 34.
29. G. R. Woodward *The Adoration of The Kings, Depicted by The Great Masters*, London, 1924, p. 20.
30. The National Gallery has no record of the bequest, which was made subject to the condition that the painting was 'never to leave England on any consideration'. The picture was probably not accepted by the Gallery.
31. G. R. Woodward *The Babe of Bethlehem, Being some Christmas Carols*, London, 1923, p. 18.
32. G. R. Woodward *Low Sunday at Gangra of Paphlagonia*, London, 1924, p. 7.
33. The letters and papers relating to the award of the degree of Doctor of Music to GRW are all kept in the Lambeth Palace Library, Davidson Papers. Vol. 404 ff 47–61. The Sir Walter referred to here is Sir Walter Parratt, whom Davidson usually consulted on petitions such as this; terminal illness prevented his involvement in this particular case. Hugh Allen, subsequently knighted, was Organist at New College, Oxford, at this time, and later occupied the Chair of Music in the University of Oxford.

## Chapter Eight: The Final Years 1925–1934

1. See Anselm Hughes, Op. Cit., p. 21.
2. J. H. Arnold, in *Walter Howard Frere, Bishop of Truro*, ed. C. S. Phillips, London, 1947, p. 169.
3. Sydney Nicholson, in the above work, p. 161.
4. Letter to the author, June 7th 1982.
5. The manuscript, together with the three letters mentioned later in the chapter, are in the possession of Mrs Ann Duff.

6. See Hughes, Op. Cit., pps. 36–37.
7. These fairly numerous booklets are now comparatively rare; it is possible that others too were printed which are unknown both to library catalogues and to the present author.
8. G. R. Woodward *Sanctorale Parvulum, or Some Greek Church Versicles Rimed in English Measures*, London, 1925, p. 9.
9. G. R. Woodward *Miscellaneous Verse Sacred and Secular*, London, 1928, p. 17.
10. Ibid., p. 14.
11. Ibid., p. 20.
12. Letter to the author, January 5th 1983.
13. Further letter to the author, undated, 1983.
14. See Jo Park *Athelstan Riley*, Truro, 1982, p. 35.
15. See Ibid., p. 36.
16. GRW to Athelstan Riley, January 27th, 1930, Riley Papers, MS 2348, f.4, Lambeth Palace Library.
17. See Jo Park, Op. Cit., p. 11.
18. *The Cambridge Carol Book*, p. 59.
19. See Colin Stephenson, Op. Cit., p. 139.
20. Two of the seven booklets produced in the following year 1929, use the same description, but it did not occur again in the (presumed) last six booklets, which were printed in 1931.
21. 'A.M.D.G. IN HONOREM GLORIOSAE MARIAE SEMPER VIRGINIS ET IN PIAM MEMORIAM GEORGE RATCLIFFE WOODWARD PRESBYTER SACRAE MUSICAE DOCTORIS OBIT ANNO DOMINI MXCXXXIV IN ANNO OCTOGESIMO SEXTO AETATIS R.I.P.' – 'To the greater glory of God, in honour of the glorious ever-virgin Mary, and in devout memory of George Ratcliffe Woodward, Priest and Doctor of Music, who died in the year of Our Lord 1934 at the age of eighty-six. May he rest in peace.'
22. 'Beneath this sign tau lies George Ratcliffe Woodward, an unworthy priest.' (For *signa tau* see the Vulgate translation of Ezekiel 9:4)
23. G. R. Woodward *Carols for Easter and Ascension-tide*, London, 1894, p. 16.

## Conclusion

1. C. S. Phillips, Op. Cit., p. 144.
2. Mervyn Horder, Op. Cit., p. 52.
3. Anselm Hughes, Op. Cit., p. 27.
4. Letter to the author, April 26th, 1995.
5. The Revd H. H. Woodward was a member of the Worcestershire family of Woodwards of Arley Castle, whom GRW supposed to be distant relatives.
6. Kenneth Long, Op. Cit., p. 401.
7. 'H.A.K.' in the *Eastern Daily Press* for March 8th 1934.

# APPENDIX

## A CHRONOLOGICAL LIST OF THE PUBLISHED WORKS
## OF G. R. WOODWARD

NOTE: *It is possible that GRW may have published other minor works which are not found in the catalogues of the British Library or of other libraries. It also seems that he occasionally published poems and translations in various journals; these are not listed here.*

CAROLS FOR CHRISTMAS-TIDE. COMPILED AND ARRANGED BY ... SERIES I,
Pickering and Chatto, London, 1892.

CAROLS FOR CHRISTMAS-TIDE. COMPILED AND ARRANGED BY ... SERIES II,
Pickering and Chatto, London, 1893.

CAROLS FOR EASTER AND ASCENSION-TIDE. COMPILED AND ARRANGED BY ...
Pickering and Chatto, London, 1894.

THE CANTICLES AT MATTINS AND EVENSONG, POINTED TO THE EIGHT
GREGORIAN TONES AS GIVEN IN THE SARUM TONALE. BY THE REVD G. H.
PALMER AND ...,
George Bell and Sons, London, 1894.

HYMNS AND CAROLS FOR CHRISTMAS-TIDE. EDITED BY ...,
H. Grice, London, 1897.

LEGENDS OF THE SAINTS.
Kegan Paul and Co., London, 1898.

A SERMON (ON MATTHEW XXV.40) PREACHED AT ST. BARNABAS, PIMLICO.
JULY 15TH 1900.
Privately Printed, London, 1900.

EASTER CAROLS. TRANSLATED BY ....
H. Grice, London, 1900.

THE COWLEY CAROL BOOK FOR CHRISTMAS, EASTER, AND ASCENSIONTIDE.
COMPILED AND ARRANGED BY ....
A. R. Mowbray, Oxford, 1901.

> THE COWLEY CAROL BOOK. REVISED AND ENLARGED.
> A. R. Mowbray, Oxford, 1902.

> THE COWLEY CAROL BOOK, SECOND SERIES.
> A. R. Mowbray, Oxford, 1919.

> THE COWLEY CAROL BOOK. COMPLETE EDITION.
> A. R. Mowbray, London, 1947.

THE SEVEN SLEEPERS OF EPHESUS.
Privately Printed, London, 1902.

POEMATA.
Longmans and Co., London, 1903.

SONGS OF SYON. A COLLECTION OF HYMNS & SACRED POEMS MOSTLY
TRANSLATED FROM ANCIENT GREEK, LATIN AND GERMAN SOURCES.
Schott, London, 1904.

> SONGS OF SYON. ... 2ND ED.
> Schott, London, 1904.
>
> SONGS OF SYON. A COLLECTION OF PSALMS, HYMNS, & SPIRITUAL SONGS
> FOR PUBLIC AND PRIVATE USE. 3RD ED.
> Schott, London, 1908.
>
> SONGS OF SYON. A COLLECTION OF PSALMS, HYMNS, & SPIRITUAL SONGS
> SET, FOR THE MOST PART, TO THEIR ANCIENT AND PROPER TUNES.
> 3RD ED.
> Schott, London, 1910.
>
> SONGS OF SYON. ... 4TH ED.,
> Schott, London, 1923.

PIAE CANTIONES. A COLLECTION OF CHURCH & SCHOOL SONGS, CHIEFLY
ANCIENT SWEDISH, ORIGINALLY PUBLISHED IN AD1582 BY THEODORIC PETRI
OF NYLAND, REVISED AND RE-EDITED, WITH PREFACE AND EXPLANATORY
NOTES, BY ...
Chiswick Press, for P.M.M.S., London, 1910.

COCK ROBIN AND JENNY WREN. A BALLAD FOR CHILDREN.
Chiswick Press, for Herbert and Daniel, London, 1911.

GOLDEN LAYS OF GOLDEN DAYS.
Chiswick Press, for Herbert and Daniel, London, 1911.

FOURTEEN ANCIENT FAUXBOURDONS (MAGNIFICAT) ED. E. W. GOLDSMITH
AND ...
P.M.M.S., London, 1912.

CUPID AND PSYCHE. FROM THE LATIN OF APULEIUS. DONE INTO ENGLISH VERSE
BY ...,
Chiswick Press, for Herbert and Daniel, London, 1912.

ST JOHN OF DAMASCUS. CANON FOR THE REPOSE OF THE MOTHER OF GOD.
DONE INTO ENGLISH VERSE BY ...,
Re-printed from The Dublin Review, 1913.

ST JOHN DAMASCENE. BALAAM AND JOASAPH. WITH AN ENGLISH TRANSLATION
BY ... AND H. MATTINGLY.
Loeb Classical Library, London, 1914.

THE ACATHIST HYMN. DONE INTO ENGLISH VERSE BY ... EDITED BY W. J.
BIRKBECK AND ...,
Longmans, Green and Co., 1917.

THE MOST HOLY MOTHER OF GOD IN THE SONGS OF THE EASTERN CHURCH.
TRANSLATED FROM THE GREEK BY ...,
Faith Press, London, 1919.

SAINT GEORGE MEGLOMARTYR IN TWENTY HYMNS OF THE HOLY AND
ORTHODOX EASTERN CHURCH, NOW FIRST DONE INTO ENGLISH VERSE BY ...,
Faith Press, London, 1919.

AN ITALIAN CAROL BOOK: BEING A SELECTION OF LAUDE SPIRITUALI OF THE XVIth AND XVIIth CENTURIES. EDITED BY C. WOOD AND ...,
Faith Press, London, 1920.

HYMNS, FROM SONGS OF SYON. HYMNS SET TO THE OLD FRENCH PSALM-TUNES AND CANTICLES OF THE 16TH CENTURY (FOR KING'S COLLEGE CHAPEL),
S.P.C.K., Cambridge, 1920.

HYMNS OF THE GREEK CHURCH,
S.P.C.K., London, 1922.

CAROLS FOR YULE-TIDE,
Privately Printed, Highgate, 1922.

THE BABE OF BETHLEHAM. BEING SOME CHRISTMAS CAROLS,
Privately Printed, Highgate, 1923.

THE MOTHER OF MY LORD, OR CAROLS FOR OUR LADY,
Privately Printed, Highgate, 1923.

THE CAMBRIDGE CAROL BOOK. BEING FIFTY-TWO SONGS FOR CHRISTMAS, EASTER, AND OTHER SEASONS. EDITED BY CHARLES WOOD AND ...,
S.P.C.K., London, 1924.

GOOD FRIDAY AND EASTER DAY COUPLETS,
Primately Printed, Highgate, 1924.

LOW SUNDAY AT GANGRA OF PAPHLOGONIA,
Privately Printed, Highgate, 1924.

ACTA SANCTORUM. BEING XII POEMS BY ...,
A. R. Mowbray, London, 1924.

THE ADORATION OF THE KINGS. EDITED BY ...,
The Medici Society, London, 1924.

CARMINA PASCHALIA: OR, CAROLS FOR EASTER-TIDE,
Privately Printed, Highgate, 1924.

GREEK ANTHOLOGY. LOVE-EPIGRAMS TURNED INTO ENGLISH VERSE BY ...,
Privately Printed, Highgate, 1924.

DOMESTICA. BEING GREEK EPIGRAMS ENGLISHED BY ...,
Privately Printed, Highgate, 1925.

THEOKRITOS. IDYLLION XI KYKLOPS POLYPNEUMOS. DRAWN INTO ENGLISH VERSE BY ...,
Privately Printed, Highgate, 1925.

SANCTORALE PARVULUM. BEING CERTAIN GREEK CHURCH VERSICLES RIMED IN ENGLISH MEASURES BY ...,
Privately Printed, Highgate, 1925.

THE STORY OF KLEOBIS AND BITON TOLD IN ENGLISH RIME BY ...,
Privately Printed, Highgate, 1926.

GREEK ANTHOLOGY. BEAUTY-EPIGRAMS TURNED INTO ENGLISH VERSE BY ...
Privately Printed, Highgate, 1926.

CERTAIN OF AESOP'S FABLES. DRAWN INTO ENGLISH VERSE BY ...,
Privately Printed, Highgate, 1926.

TRANSLATIONS OF ITALIAN, FRENCH AND GERMAN POEMS BY ...,
Privately Printed, Highgate, 1928.

MISCELLANEOUS VERSE SACRED AND SECULAR,
Privately Printed, Highgate, 1928.

SPRING-TIME SONGS TRANSLATED FROM THE GREEK BY ...,
Privately Printed, Highgate, 1928.

TART AND HOMELY GIBES OF GREEK EPIGRAMMATISTS ENGLISHED BY ...,
Privately Printed, Highgate, 1928.

GLEANINGS FROM ANCIENT OLIVE-YARDS GREEK AND ROMAN,
Privately Printed, Highgate, 1928.

CANTICA SPIRITUALIA, TURNED INTO ENGLISH VERSE BY ...,
Privately Printed, Highgate, 1928.

A BUNCH OF GRAPES FROM ANCIENT GREEK VINEYARDS CRUSHED INTO
ENGLISH MEASURES BY ...,
Privately Printed, Highgate, 1929.

GREEK ANTHOLOGY. EPIGRAMMATA HEROICA DRAWN INTO ENGLISH VERSE
BY ...,
Privately Printed, Highgate, 1929.

THE STORY OF ARION AND THE DOLPHIN,
Privately Printed, Highgate, 1929.

GREEK WITTICISMS TOLD IN ENGLISH VERSE,
Privately Printed, Highgate, 1929.

GREEK EPIGRAMS ON AND BY FAMOUS POETS AND MUSICIANS. ENGLISHED
BY ...,
Privately Printed, Highgate, 1929.

SOME REMNANTS OF GREEK COMEDY ENGLISHED BY ...,
Privately Printed, Highgate, 1929.

ST HALWARD THE MARTYR: ALSO TWO MORAL FABLES, BY ...,
Privately Printed, Highgate, 1929.

TALES OF SEA-SORROW FROM THE GREEK ANTHOLOGY ENGLISHED BY ...,
Privately Printed, Highgate, 1931.

A GARLAND OF SPIRITUAL FLOWERS WOVEN BY ...,
Privately Printed, Highgate, 1931.

FIVE AND FORTY EXAMPLES OF THE EPIGRAM SEPULCHRAL TURNED OUT OF
GREEK INTO ENGLISH VERSE BY ...,
Privately Printed, Highgate, 1931.

EPIGRAMS OF SAPPHO AND OTHER FAMOUS GREEK LYRIC POETESSES ENGLISHED
BY ...,
Privately Printed, Highgate, 1931.

GREEK EPIGRAMS, RELIGIOUS AND DEDICATORY PART I. TURNED INTO ENGLISH
VERSE BY ...,
Privately Printed, Highgate, 1931.

GREEK EPIGRAMS, RELIGIOUS AND DEDICATORY PART II. TURNED INTO ENGLISH
VERSE BY ...,
Privately Printed, Highgate, 1931.

GREEK EPIGRAMS OF TIMON, DIOGENES & OTHERS TURNED INTO ENGLISH
VERSE BY ...,
Privately Printed, Highgate, 1931.

# A Note on The Theodore Trust and its Founder

The publication of this book has been made possible by financial assistance from The Theodore Trust, which was established by the Revd Alan Vincent Carefull in 1992. The object of the trust is 'The advancement of the Christian Religion', and one of the means by which this purpose is fulfilled is by facilitating the publication of appropriate religious literature.

Like George Ratcliffe Woodward, Alan Carefull came from the prosperous middle classes of Liverpool. He was educated at Liverpool College, before winning an Exhibition to Magdalen College Oxford, where he read Modern History and afterwards Theology. He prepared for the Anglican priesthood at St Stephen's House, Oxford, and like so many other ordinands he was deeply influenced by the then Principal, The Revd Arthur Couratin. After curacies at St Augustine's, Tonge Moor, Bolton, and St John's, Tue Brook, Liverpool, he returned to St Stephen's House as Vice-Principal, and remained there for five years before becoming Vicar of the city-centre parish of St John's, Newcastle upon Tyne, where he initiated a noteworthy re-ordering of the church. Eight years in Newcastle were followed by a further eight years as Administrator of the Shrine of Our Lady of Walsingham, and on relinquishing this work in 1981 he continued to live in Norfolk, assisting in local parishes and latterly in the chaplaincy at Norwich Prison.

Alan Carefull had been drawn towards Anglo-catholicism as a young man, just as Woodward had been, and again like him he was a steadfast supporter of orthodox belief, a lover of dignified worship, and a notable example of faithfulness and strict discipline in the pursuit of the spiritual life. His self-discipline was marked, and although he was a person of strong and definite opinion, it was rare indeed for him to betray any sign of irritation or annoyance. Similarly, he hardly ever spoke of anyone in a critical or unkind way. He shared Woodward's interest in hymnology and in the tradition of the Eastern Church, as well as his enthusiasm for classical music and good wine. His humour was less hidden

163

2

than that of Woodward; he was an accomplished mimic, and had a tremendous and liberating sense of fun. No one was allowed to take themselves too seriously. He had an enthusiastic and infectious interest in Holy Scripture and in east-European history, but perhaps his greatest strength lay in his ability as a teacher and preacher. He took delight in the practice of these arts, sometimes jokingly expressing the fear that his excessive pleasure in preaching amounted to a sin!

Again like Woodward, Alan Carefull came to hold a great veneration for the Blessed Virgin Mary, and a deep awareness of her unique place in the pattern of redemption. Both men worked in Walsingham, Woodward as parish priest in the 1880s and Alan Carefull as Administrator of the Shrine nearly a century later, and this Norfolk village so long associated with the Mother of the Incarnate Word came to hold a very special place in the affection and imagination of both men. But Alan Carefull did not live to see old-age, as Woodward did; tragically, he was killed in a motor accident on June 10th 1992 at the age of sixty-eight, when returning home from duties at Norwich Prison. The remains of both men rest far away from their native Liverpool, in the North Norfolk countryside. May their souls rest in light and peace.

J.E.B.

# INDEX